Trade in the
Common Market Countries

A. E. WALSH, M.B.E
JOHN PAXTON, Ph.D

A. E. Walsh & Partners Ltd

Designed and produced by Hutchinson Benham Limited
178–202 Great Portland Street, London W.1

First published 1965

338.91
W

Further copies of TRADE IN THE COMMON MARKET COUNTRIES are obtainable from your bookseller, or from:

A. E. Walsh & Partners Ltd., 'Euromarket Surveys' Division: 92 New Cavendish Street, London W.1, England

Printed in Great Britain by Benham and Company Limited, Colchester

CONTENTS

Introduction   5

The Common Market—an historical note   7

PART I

Tables, under 180 commodity headings, showing total imports, the supplying countries' share of those imports and the Export:Import ratio for each commodity.

	Preface	9
	Index	10
1	France	11
2	West Germany	17
3	Italy	23
4	The Netherlands	29
5	Belgium/Luxembourg	35

PART II

Trading accounts, extracted from Input/Output statistics, for about eighteen main industries in the Common Market countries.

	Preface	41
	Index	42
1	France	43
2	West Germany	53
3	Italy	61
4	The Netherlands	71
5	Belgium/Luxembourg	79

PART III

Production figures for some fifty basic commodities in the Common Market, together with each country's share of the total figures.

	Preface	91
	Index	92
	Tables	93

PART IV—*overleaf*

PART IV

Supplementary notes on production, consumption, imports and exports in Common Market countries for some important commodities.

	Preface	95
	Index	96
1	Automobiles	97
2	Motor car accessories	98
3	Non-ferrous metals (aluminium, copper)	98
4	Plastics	102
5	Pulp and paper	104
6	Consumer durables (domestic and office machinery)	106
7	Leather footwear	107
8	Stockings	108
9	Knitwear	109

Sources of the statistical information   111

INTRODUCTION

For seventy years, until 1932, Britain was a free trade country. That period saw a great surge of British investment abroad and the opening of her doors to free and cheap imports from the whole world as a means of getting returns from that investment. One of the consequences was that Britain also developed a trading economy and outlook which accepted imports as a matter of course and provided wholesale channels of distribution for imported manufactures on a scale unparalleled in any of the European countries, whose growing industrialization was geared to high tariffs against imports.

Britain's policy on exports was conditioned to a great extent over this period by her trade with far-distant countries. To the average manufacturer, exporting meant selling to Australia, New Zealand, and Canada, to India, China, Ceylon, Burma and other Far-Eastern countries, to South Africa and South America. These were the halcyon days when the great pioneer merchants in wholesaling and retailing were setting up their establishments in every corner of the globe, complemented with their own buying offices in Britain or using the services of the complex of indent merchants who made the trading of the manufacturer easy. During this time, Europe ranked low as a market for British manufactured goods. The trade was left to Europeans themselves.

All this has changed. For a variety of reasons, mostly economic and political, we can no longer depend on far-distant markets to pay our way. Late, and in many ways ill-equipped for the task, Britain must, within the next ten years, establish herself completely in the European markets. Moreover, she must do so with methods which are very different from those which her manufacturers have used for exporting in the past, and with the additional handicap of a discriminatory tariff against her products in the six largest countries.

We have compiled this work with one important object in view; to assist actual and potential exporters in their assessments of trading conditions and possibilities in the Common Market countries.

We have considered this task in terms of statistics—of what France, Italy, West Germany, Netherlands and Belgium/Luxembourg import, where these imports come from, and what relation their imports bear to their exports of similar commodities. The four Parts are complementary, and the information in them should be considered together. Details are given under about 180 different commodity headings, so that TRADE IN THE COMMON MARKET COUNTRIES is a book of easy reference to everyone concerned with exporting to and from Europe.

The figures contained in this book are made available in this form for the first time in the United Kingdom or elsewhere. While the information has been compiled from official sources and is completely authentic, no Government or private publication has ever analysed trade figures in a way which conveys such a wealth of detail in such small compass.

The main emphasis in the tables is on what each country buys from suppliers outside its own territory, trade which is, therefore, available to any country that can compete in price, quality, design, delivery and service with other external suppliers. In addition, the tables show the extent to which, for these 180 commodities, each country exports more or less than it imports and, therefore, *prima facie*, whether the market is a 'hard' or a 'soft' one for imports.

The tables presented in this study should be of considerable value, we hope, for recognizing the pattern of the movement of goods going into and coming out of the various countries of the Common Market in terms of what has been their 'external' trade, but what will eventually be the 'domestic' trade of the Common Market as a single trading unit. Patterns of trade of the kind set out in the tables are subject to changes, but such changes will, in all probability, only be marginal and unlikely to affect any assessment of the main trends to any marked degree. All the figures have been rounded off and are to that extent approximate. Intra-Community trade, i.e. trade between one country of the Common Market and another, has been treated as the imports and exports of each of the member countries in the same way as their trade with third countries.

Further valuable information is contained in the section of the book which analyses recently published Input/Output Statistical Tables.

Input/Output Tables provide a statistical analysis of the economic inter-relationships of industries in a country. Their main purpose is to provide a basis from which to project economic forecast. In this book, the information has been distilled from a mass of statistical data in such a way as to treat each national industry as a business undertaking. Each Input/Output Table has been reduced to the form of a commercial trading account. On the debit side are shown the principal cost components—raw materials, value added in wages, employers' social service payments, depreciation, indirect taxation and miscellaneous including profit. On the credit side are shown the values of sales to other industries and for private and public consumption; sales for fixed asset formation and for export, together with stock variations. Imports of similar products are added to the total resources and the two sides of the account balance. By deducting exports, the value of the apparent domestic consumption is shown.

The information set out in this section of the book will prove invaluable to any manufacturing firm in the industries covered in comparing its performance with the situation in the industry as a whole in each Common Market country.

With its clear presentation of a mass of information concerning most basic commodities, we trust that TRADE IN THE COMMON MARKET COUNTRIES will be recognized and accepted as a unique and valuable work of reference by those concerned with exporting and all students of European economics and the pattern of world trade.

A. E. Walsh

September 1965

John Paxton

THE COMMON MARKET
An historical note

The Common Market began on 1 January 1958 following the signing of the Treaty of Rome on 25 March 1957. Its six member countries are France, West Germany, Italy, the Netherlands, Belgium and Luxembourg, of which the last three were already members of a Customs Union of their own, Benelux.

The origins, evolution and aims of the Common Market have been the subject of many authoritative works and are outside the scope of this book. The measures initiated by Britain to become associated with the Common Market first in the unsuccessful negotiations to form a Free Trade Area in association with the Common Market, and second to join the Common Market as full members with the other members of the European Free Trade Association which was set up in 1960 between Britain, Norway, Sweden, Denmark, Switzerland, Austria and Portugal, with Finland co-operating, now form part of history rather than current economic research.

One of the first objectives of the Treaty of Rome was the creation of a Customs Union, in which all the member countries abolished tariffs and quantitative restrictions in trade amongst themselves, and at the same time established a unified tariff on imports from all non-member countries, with the exception of countries, notably their associated overseas territories, covered by special conventions.

The Common Market has accelerated its original time table for the progressive reduction and the final abolition of tariffs between member countries and for establishing the final levels of their Common External Tariff. If there is no delay arising from differences which have developed, mainly on political issues, towards the final stage of the implementation of the Treaty of Rome, there will be complete free trade between France, West Germany, Italy, the Netherlands, Belgium and Luxembourg by January 1967. Goods entering any of the Common Market countries from the rest of the world will pay the unified rate of duty whatever their destination within the Common Market.

In other words, the Common Market countries will, in the near future, be able to buy one another's products at duty-free prices while suppliers from the rest of the world will have to surmount a tariff barrier of anything from about 10 to 25 per cent on what they want to sell in the Common Market.

Against this, in a Europe in which living standards and incomes are rising rapidly, people will have more money to spend on the commodities associated with higher living standards. They will need more and better clothes, household equipment, radio and television sets, washing machines, refrigerators, carpets, cars and cameras, regardless of where these come from so long as they are offered competitive value for their money. The Common Market manufacturers, too, will need more machines and raw materials to fulfil the requirements of their domestic market.

Trade in the modern world flows increasingly in all directions. Ships bringing European products to Britain will pass other ships taking similar British products to Europe. How far the ships passing in either direction will be fully loaded or in ballast will depend as much upon the attitude of individual manufacturers towards getting their share of foreign trade as upon economic climate or the impact of tariffs.

PART I

Tables, under 180 commodity headings, showing total imports, the supplying countries share of those imports and the Export: Import ratio for each commodity.

PREFACE

These tables show at a glance where each country in the Common Market buys the greater part of its supplies of 180 different industrial commodities. In the tables, the countries supplying the bulk of the total imports are given; but supplementary notes indicate, in exceptional cases, other significant sources.

An important feature of the following tables is the Export:Import Ratio given against each commodity. This figure in a measurement in economic terms of the relative strength of the domestic industry in terms of its ability to export or its dependence on imports, and should be a useful aid in the task of locating potentially profitable markets among the industries listed. The figures in these tables are for the year 1963.

INDEX

	France	West Germany	Italy	Nether-lands	Belgium/ Luxem-bourg
	page	*page*	*page*	*page*	*page*
BASE METALS Iron and Steel Products, Non-Ferrous Metals (Aluminium, Copper, Lead, Magnesium, Nickel, Zinc, Other)	11	17	23	29	35
BOOKS AND PERIODICALS	15	21	27	33	39
CHEMICALS AND CHEMICAL PRODUCTS Artists' Colours, Dyestuffs, Paints and Varnishes, Perfumery, Polishes and Waxes, Soap, Washing Preparations	11	17	23	29	35
CLOTHING Corsetry, Footwear, Stockings, Outerwear—various, Underwear—various	14	20	26	32	38
CLOCKS AND WATCHES	14	20	26	32	38
CONSUMER DURABLES	14	20	26	32	38
CUTLERY	14	20	26	32	38
EARTH-MOVING EQUIPMENT	13	19	25	31	37
ELECTRICAL EQUIPMENT AND SUPPLIES	12	18	24	30	36
ELECTRICAL PLANT	12	18	24	30	36
FABRICS, WOVEN AND KNITTED Cotton, Knitted, Linen, Narrow, Synthetic, Woollen	14	20	26	32	38
FACTORY PLANT AND EQUIPMENT Engineering Supplies, Industrial Machinery, Production Machinery	12	18	24	30	36
FERTILIZERS Nitrogenous, Phosphatic, Potassic	11	17	23	29	35
FOOD MANUFACTURES	15	21	27	33	39
HOUSEHOLD EQUIPMENT	14	20	26	32	38
METAL MANUFACTURES	14	20	26	32	38
MISCELLANEOUS MANUFACTURES	15	21	27	33	39
OFFICE EQUIPMENT Accounting Machines, Duplicating Machines, Electronic Machines, Punched Card Machines, Typewriters	13	19	25	31	37
OPTICAL AND PHOTOGRAPHIC GOODS	13	19	25	31	37
PAPER	12	18	24	30	36
PHARMACEUTICALS	11	17	23	29	35
PLASTICS Plastic Manufactures, Products of Condensation, Products of Polymerization	13	19	25	31	37
RADIO AND TELEVISION	15	21	27	33	39
RUBBER MANUFACTURES	14	20	26	32	38
SCIENTIFIC INSTRUMENTS	13	19	25	31	37
TOOLS AND IMPLEMENTS	13	19	25	31	37
TRANSPORT Automobiles, Automobile Accessories, Tractors	13	19	25	31	37
VENDING MACHINES	13	19	25	31	37
WEIGHING MACHINES	13	19	25	31	37
TOTAL TRADE	15	21	27	33	39

Product Group and Product	Total Imports $'000	Suppliers' Percentage Share of Imports											Export/ Import Ratio ($ million)	Notes
		U.S.	U.K.	Ger.	It.	Neth.	Bel/ Lux.	Nor.	Swe.	Den.	Switz.	Aust.		
		%	%	%	%	%	%	%	%	%	%	%		
BASE METALS														
Iron and Steel														
Blooms & Billets	42,295	–	*	66	*	*	25	1	1	–	–	–	15.5 : 42.3	(1)
Iron & Steel coils for re-rolling	46,973	*	10	24	2	9	36	–	–	–	–	1	11.0 : 47.0	(2)
Iron & Steel wire rod	16,192	–	–	67	–	–	20	–	9	–	–	–	62.0 : 16.0	
Steel Bars	43,350	–	*	78	1	*	25	–	–	–	–	–	62.0 : 43.0	
Steel Angles, Shapes and Sections	41,483	–	2	60	12	–	35	–	–	–	–	–	52.0 : 41.0	
Iron & Steel Sheet, heavy	52,133	–	8	60	4	2	25	–	–	–	–	–	15.0 : 52.0	
Iron & Steel Sheet, medium	10,483	–	9	34	3	1	52	–	–	–	–	–	12.0 : 10.5	
Iron & Steel Sheet, thin	54,051	–	1	31	2	3	56	1	*	–	–	–	140.0 : 54.0	
Iron Plate	20,952	*	10	22	7	13	48	–	–	–	–	–	72.0 : 21.0	
Iron & Steel Wire	4,929	*	*	81	*	1	15	–	*	–	1	–	14.0 : 5.0	
Seamless Tubes and Pipes	5,313	–	*	78	–	2	2	–	18	–	–	–	9.0 : 5.3	
Welded Tubes and Pipes	18,064	7	7	56	*	2	8	–	13	*	3	*	79.0 : 18.0	
Tube & Pipe Fittings	8,946	14	9	44	2	6	3	*	3	*	14	1	12.5 : 9.0	
Non-Ferrous Metals														
Copper Bars, Rods, etc.	3,498	4	5	29	1	16	32	1	–	–	7	4	5.6 : 3.5	
Copper Plates, Sheets, Strip, etc.	3,617	47	3	8	20	6	6	–	–	–	5	–	6.9 : 3.6	
Copper Tubes & Pipes	3,631	3	16	46	2	12	16	–	–	–	2	3	3.8 : 3.6	
Nickel Bars, Rods etc.	1,895	23	53	10	–	3	*	–	7	–	3	–	1.0 : 1.9	
Nickel Strip, Powders, etc.	1,800	12	46	34	–	*	4	–	–	–	1	–	0.9 : 1.8	
Unwrought Aluminium	25,628	11	*	*	–	–	–	–	–	–	*	–	57.0 : 25.6	(3)
Aluminium Bars, Rods, etc.	2,732	13	11	19	3	4	28	1	–	–	9	–	1.9 : 2.7	(4)
Aluminium Plates, Sheet, Strip etc.	9,209	6	5	47	5	9	11	*	*	–	10	–	6.9 : 9.2	
Lead, Unwrought	11,921	*	*	7	–	1	32	–	–	–	–	–	5.0 : 12.0	(5)
Zinc, Unwrought	4,453	–	*	4	–	6	53	12	–	–	–	–	3.0 : 4.5	(6)
Tin, Unwrought	29,146	–	11	*	–	7	28	–	–	–	–	–	Neg. : 29.0	(7)
Magnesium, Unwrought and Wrought	1,753	25	32	1	10	–	–	12	–	–	–	–	Neg. : 1.7	
Other Non-ferrous metal products	12,576	16	19	3	–	5	23	–	–	–	–	–	3.3 : 12.5	
CHEMICALS AND CHEMICAL PRODUCTS														
Mineral and Chemical Fertilizers														
Nitrogenous	6,950	–	–	12	5	–	76	1	–	–	5	–	23.0 : 7.0	
Phosphatic	22,342	–	–	10	–	25	50	–	–	–	–	–	6.0 : 22.3	(8)
Potassic	3,118	–	–	7	–	–	93	–	–	–	–	–	36.0 : 3.0	
Paints & Varnishes	9,571	15	8	36	2	23	10	*	1	*	3	–	9.6 : 9.5	
Synthetic Organic Dyestuffs	25,412	4	10	37	2	2	4	–	–	*	39	–	13.6 : 25.0	
Artists Colours	252	3	27	30	3	26	–	–	–	–	–	–	0.3 : 0.3	
Soap	866	6	10	15	1	26	41	–	–	–	*	–	8.4 : 0.8	
Perfumery & Cosmetics	2,418	12	13	35	11	9	11	–	–	–	8	–	48.0 : 2.4	
Polishes, Waxes, etc.	2,700	6	4	28	3	2	43	–	–	*	13	–	1.8 : 2.7	
Surface-acting Washing preps.	6,738	20	5	47	2	1	13	–	2	–	10	–	9.2 : 6.7	
Pharmaceutical Products														
Medicaments	5,556	12	8	12	7	8	10	–	2	16	11	–	74.0 : 5.0	
Padding, Gauze, etc.	98	45	6	12	13	–	22	–	–	–	–	–	3.0 : 0.1	
Disinfectants, Insecticides, etc.	5,989	11	9	43	8	7	6	–	1	1	13	–	18.0 : 6.0	

Where a dash is shown imports are nil or negligible.   * Where an asterisk is shown imports are less than 1 per cent.

Notes: Other exporting countries include:

(1) Canada 2%   (3) Cameroons 81%, Canada 6%.   (5) North Africa 50%.   (7) Malaysia 33%, Indonesia 5%, China 9%.

(2) U.S.S.R. 13%, Japan 3%.   (4) Canada 5%, U.S.S.R. 5%.   (6) Congo, Rhodesia, Nyasaland 16%.   (8) North Africa 15%.

Product Group and Product	Total Imports $'000	Suppliers' Percentage Share of Imports											Export/Import Ratio ($ million)	Notes
		U.S.	U.K.	Ger.	It.	Neth.	Bel/Lux.	Nor.	Swe.	Den.	Switz.	Aust.		
		%	%	%	%	%	%	%	%	%	%	%	%	
PAPER														
Kraft Paper	23,741	7.5	*	1	*	*	*	3	46	—	—	—	4.0 : 24.0	(1)
Building Board	5,146	4	*	32	*	2	6	*	27	—	*	7	3.0 : 5.2	(2)
Newsprint	10,779	2	*	3	—	2	6	15	44	—	—	—	1.0 : 10.8	(3)
FACTORY PLANT & EQUIPMENT														
Industrial Machinery														
Steam Boilers	3,713	16	4	40	2	1	19	—	—	2	16	—	5.2 : 3.7	
Aux. Steam Plant	863	2	17	60	*	*	1	—	16	—	2	—	4.1 : 0.9	
Refrigerating Equipment	8,545	19	5	21	35	*	4	2	6	2	2	*	7.0 : 8.5	
Air Conditioning Equipment	3,376	68	9	5	12	1	2	—	1	*	1	—	5.0 : 3.4	
Heating Plant	22,536	19	11	32	17	6	3	*	4	3	4	*	37.0 : 23.0	
Pumping M/c for Liquids	18,995	22	13	39	6	3	4	1	3	4	3	1	26.0 : 19.0	
Pumping M/c for Air and Vacuum	20,409	20	13	22	6	1	8	*	3	1	22	1	10.0 : 20.0	
Centrifugal M/c.	11,346	17	10	41	6	2	5	*	6	2	7	*	14.5 : 11.0	
Production Machinery														
Pulp & Paper Machinery	9,824	33	5	33	10	*	2	*	10	—	2	*	12.0 : 10.0	
Textile Weaving and Knitting Machinery	23,116	6	10	27	10	—	9	—	1	*	33	*	6.5 : 23.0	
Machine Tools for Metal Working	95,790	14	10	44	7	2	5	*	2	*	11	*	59.0 : 96.0	
Rolling Mills Equipment	10,470	8	14	50	3	—	7	—	2	—	*	15	12.0 : 10.5	
Welding Plant	638	10	*	85	—	—	1	—	1	—	*	—	1.5 : 0.6	
Spinning and Doubling M/c.	15,294	6	13	32	15	*	15	—	—	—	18	5	27.0 : 15.0	
Packaging Machinery & Bottling Plant	17,158	14	7	43	5	4	6	—	7	—	12	—	10.0 : 17.0	
Pneumatic M/c. Tools	10,856	28	5	32	—	*	17	—	10	—	*	*	1.9 : 10.8	
Engineering Supplies														
Sandpaper, Emery Paper, etc.	3,696	20	2	57	9	*	*	—	1	*	9	—	1.9 : 3.7	
Refractory Goods	1,743	14	5	58	*	4	3	1	—	—	*	12	0.9 : 1.7	
Fabricated Asbestos	1,626	12	50	17	*	6	1	—	*	—	2	8	2.2 : 1.6	
Ball Bearings	18,476	36	8	30	7	*	*	—	5	*	6	1	12.5 : 18.0	
Rubber Belting	2,017	20	16	22	16	9	21	—	2	*	2	*	6.6 : 2.0	
Textile Belting	559	7	39	16	1	1	31	—	2	—	3	—	0.4 : 0.6	
Transmission Shafts, Gears, etc.	31,847	22	17	41	4	1	5	*	2	1	4	*	19.0 : 31.0	
Taps, Cocks, Valves, etc.	26,872	21	12	42	5	5	3	*	1	3	4	*	27.0 : 27.0	
Metal Bottle Stoppers	959	6	24	12	15	35	4	—	—	*	—	3	3.7 : 1.7	
ELECTRICAL PLANT														
Generators, Motors, etc.	27,329	22	8	31	8	4	7	—	6	1	9	1	65.0 : 27.0	
Electrical Circuit Apparatus	36,583	39	7	26	10	5	2	*	1	*	8	*	61.0 : 36.0	
ELECTRICAL EQUIPMENT														
Insulating Cable and Wire	8,389	13	7	38	9	20	*	—	5	—	1	—	26.0 : 8.4	
Insulating Fittings	2,395	14	3	36	5	17	8	—	—	—	9	1	6.3 : 2.4	
Electrical Carbons	3,451	11	2	45	12	*	*	—	—	—	*	—	8.7 : 3.5	
Electric/Electronic Measuring Apparatus	46,878	56	11	16	1	4	1	*	1	1	5	*	18.0 : 47.0	
Electro-Magnets	2,555	42	9	26	6	3	1	—	5	—	5	*	2.5 : 2.5	
Electric Filament Lamps	6,710	29	8	26	—	22	1	—	—	—	2	*	5.7 : 6.7	
Accumulators	1,350	20	13	48	2	1	2	—	*	—	9	1	6.9 : 1.3	
Batteries	1,011	20	37	21	—	1	—	—	—	13	*	—	9.5 : 1.0	
Thermionic Cathode Ray Tubes, Transistors, etc	30,479	50	9	13	7	16	—	—	—	—	*	*	25.0 : 30.0	(4)
Electricity Supply Meters	529	6	—	2	—	—	—	—	—	—	92	—	1.4 : 0.5	

— Where a dash is shown imports are nil or negligible   * Where an asterisk is shown imports are less than 1 per cent.

Notes: Other exporting countries include:

(1) Finland 40%.   (2) Finland 10%.   (3) Finland 25%.   (4) Japan 7%

Product Group and Product	Total Imports $'000	Suppliers' Percentage Share of Imports											Export/ Import Ratio ($ million)	Notes
		U.S.	U.K.	Ger.	It.	Neth.	Bel/Lux.	Nor.	Swe.	Den.	Switz.	Aus.		
		%	%	%	%	%	%	%	%	%	%	%		
TRANSPORT EQUIPMENT														
Motor Cars	162,557	3	20	51	22	1	4	–	*	–	–	–	496 : 162	
Automobile Parts and Accessories	37,428	15	18	47	13	1	*	–	*	*	*	*	89.0 : 37.0	
Tractors	75,267	11	36	31	17	1	–	–	3	–	*	*	28.0 : 75.0	
EARTH-MOVING MACHINERY														
Excavating, Levelling, etc. Machinery	30,901	50	17	21	4	*	2	*	2	–	2	1	38.0 : 31.0	
Lifting, Handling Machinery etc.	53,254	25	14	38	4	2	4	*	4	1	3	*	58.0 : 53.0	
AUTOMATIC VENDING EQUIPMENT AND WEIGHING MACHINES														
Automatic Vending Machines	1,120	46	2	30	4	*	6	–	–	9	2	–	0.1 : 1.1	
Weighing Machines	3,576	15	1	57	5	7	5	–	*	*	8	*	2.0 : 3.6	
PHOTOGRAPHIC AND OPTICAL GOODS, SCIENTIFIC INSTRUMENTS AND SUPPLIES														
Cameras	10,067	18	4	70	*	2	–	–	*	–	1	–	1.0 : 10.0	(1)
Lenses, Unmounted and Mounted	2,527	15	6	56	2	2	34	–	–	–	7	1	4.7 : 2.5	
Microscopes	2,389	4	2	60	1	*	–	–	*	–	14	14	0.3 : 2.4	
Surveying Instruments	3,924	39	13	21	2	*	*	*	1	*	19	*	2.7 : 4.0	
Electro-Medical and X-Ray Apparatus	5,953	17	1	37	7	18	4	–	7	2	2	*	3.7 : 6.0	
Thermometers, Thermostats etc.	7,045	36	14	24	3	8	1	–	3	5	4	*	7.5 : 7.0	
Drawing Instruments	7,468	14	10	42	7	*	*	–	3	*	19	*	6.7 : 7.5	
Photographic Chemicals	777	11	7	47	8	5	20	–	–	–	–	–	0.4 : 0.7	
Photographic Films	6,396	10	2	20	10	1	53	–	*	–	*	–	11.0 : 6.4	
Photographic Paper	4,610	18	4	33	1	2	18	–	–	–	–	–	4.9 : 4.6	
PLASTICS														
Products of Condensation	30,622	20	7	33	10	5	7	*	3	*	6	*	32.0 : 30.0	
Products of Polymerisation	42,637	17	10	44	15	3	4	*	*	1	1	*	39.0 : 42.0	
Plastic Manufactures	13,652	17	8	38	14	6	10	*	*	*	3	*	21.0 : 13.0	
OFFICE EQUIPMENT														
Typewriters	13,797	12	2	22	33	6	–	–	3	–	19	–	3.0 : 14.0	
Electronic Calculating Machines	8,392	64	1	25	4	*	–	–	–	–	–	–	1.7 : 8.4	
Other Accounting Machines	32,236	11	10	17	40	4	–	*	10	*	2	*	4.2 : 3.2	
Punched Card Machines	40,024	40	16	17	7	3	*	–	7	–	–	–	36.4 : 40.0	
Duplicating Machines	2,054	*	53	24	7	*	–	–	2	12	1	–	0.8 : 2.0	
TOOLS AND IMPLEMENTS														
Hand Saws	3,980	28	7	26	*	*	6	1	15	*	3	1	1.5 : 4.0	(2)
Hand Tools, Pliers, Spanners, Snips, etc.	2,879	18	6	35	2	10	1	–	9	–	9	3	3.1 : 2.9	
Electric Hand Tools	5,066	22	7	50	3	4	*	–	1	*	14	–	2.0 : 5.0	
Other Hand Tools	4,724	24	12	34	11	2	1	–	2	*	8	*	6.4 : 4.7	

Where a dash is shown imports are nil or negligible.   * Where an asterisk is shown imports are less than 1 per cent.

Notes: Other exporting countries include:

(1) Japan 3%   (2) Canada 10%.

Product Group and Product	Total Imports ($'000)	Suppliers' Percentage Share of Imports											Export/ Import Ratio ($ million)	Notes
		U.S.	U.K.	Ger.	It.	Neth.	Bel/ Lux.	Nor.	Swe.	Den.	Switz.	Aus.		
		%	%	%	%	%	%	%	%	%	%	%		
TEXTILES AND CLOTHING														
Woven & Knitted Fabrics														
Woollen Fabrics	20,757	*	41	3	42	1	7	—	*	*	*	2	46.0 : 20.0	
Cotton Fabrics, bleached and unbleached	20,536	12	3	16	9	7	17	—	*	*	14	2	95.0 : 20.0	
Linen Fabrics	346	*	36	11	11	—	17	—	2	2	9	—	2.7 : 0.4	
Fabrics of Man-made Fibres, (Synthetic and Artificial)	26,771	4	1	30	38	6	9	—	*	*	2	1	71.0 : 27.0	
Knitted Fabrics	6,187	44	6	28	10	1	10	—	—	—	1	*	9.4 : 6.2	
Narrow Fabrics	644	32	18	30	3	*	10	—	*	*	4	—	2.5 : 0.7	
Clothing														
Leather Footwear	15,379	*	1	5	58	1	9	*	—	—	14	—	43.0 : 15.4	
Knitted Outerwear	26,768	*	6	4	81	1	2	*	*	—	*	1	48.0 : 26.8	
Knitted Underwear	1,525	6	2	27	32	*	7	—	—	—	17	*	7.5 : 1.5	
Mens Underwear	1,652	12	9	33	20	2	13	—	—	—	*	—	7.0 : 1.6	
Mens Outerwear	12,654	10	7	20	40	2	13	—	*	*	2	*	19.0 : 12.6	
Womens Outerwear	7,943	3	8	11	38	22	10	—	—	—	*	1	32.4 : 8.0	
Womens Underwear	206	18	4	20	15	1	20	—	—	—	4	1	3.5 : 0.2	
Stockings	5,910	*	2	29	57	*	1	*	—	—	*	2	7.6 : 6.0	
Corsetry	3,555	10	3	60	*	11	7	—	*	—	*	5	3.0 : 3.5	
HOUSEHOLD AND CONSUMER DURABLES														
Domestic Refrigerators	22,357	4	5	24	62	*	*	*	2	—	*	—	9.4 : 22.4	
Domestic Washing Machines	11,060	2	53	19	15	1	3	—	—	—	*	—	7.0 : 11.0	
Electric Domestic Appliances	6,538	9	24	20	8	25	3	*	2	2	4	—	7.4 : 6.5	
Carpets	8,416	1	6	23	7	3	55	—	—	*	*	1	7.9 : 8.4	
Linoleum	1,040	—	14	53	—	8	23	—	—	—	2	—	18.0 : 1.0	
Sewing Machines	19,672	18	13	42	10	*	1	—	*	*	9	*	3.1 : 19.7	
Household Glassware	7,960	2	*	35	24	*	22	*	1	*	*	5	22.0 : 8.0	
Household Chinaware	2,839	—	2	85	3	*	2	—	*	*	*	—	3.3 : 2.8	(1)
Bed and Table Linen	4,487	6	1	17	19	3	32	—	*	*	3	—	10.5 : 4.5	
Electric Razors	4,176	5	15	33	12	25	—	—	—	—	3	4	3.1 : 4.2	
Spoons and Forks	781	*	22	27	25	5	*	*	*	2	*	*	2.5 : 0.8	
Knives	678	1	20	44	16	6	*	—	1	*	8	*	2.5 : 0.7	
Scissors	184	—	5	73	15	—	—	—	—	—	—	—	0.2 : 0.2	
Aluminium Domestic Utensils	1,495	2	3	14	72	—	2	—	*	—	3	2	2.5 : 1.5	
Brushware	1,361	15	12	39	4	5	18	1	1	1	2	*	2.8 : 1.4	
WATCHES AND CLOCKS														
Watches	3,928	*	—	3	—	—	—	—	—	—	96	—	5.0 : 4.0	
Clocks	2,696	1	2	80	3	*	*	—	—	—	9	—	1.9 : 2.7	
MISCELLANEOUS METAL MANUFACTURES														
Locks, etc.	1,765	4	11	48	27	*	—	—	*	*	7	—	3.9 : 1.8	
Safes, etc.	193	8	1	81	7	*	—	—	—	—	—	—	0.5 : 0.2	
Iron and Steel Chain	5,024	18	23	37	11	1	*	—	1	*	3	—	2.7 : 5.0	
Iron and Steel Springs	2,863	17	8	59	2	2	4	—	2	—	6	—	2.5 : 2.9	
RUBBER MANUFACTURES														
Tyres	10,290	8	15	20	37	1	9	—	2	—	4	1	79.0 : 10.0	
General Rubber Manufactures	8,587	19	14	49	8	*	2	—	2	*	1	*	5.0 : 8.6	

— Where a dash is shown imports are nil or negligible.   * Where an asterisk is shown imports are less than 1 per cent.

Notes: Other exporting countries include:

    (1) Japan 6%.

Product Group and Product	Total Imports $'000	Suppliers' Percentage Share of Imports											Export/ Import Ratio ($ million)	Notes
		U.S.	U.K.	Ger	It.	Neth.	Bel/ Lux.	Nor.	Swe.	Den.	Switz.	Aus.		
		%	%	%	%	%	%	%	%	%	%	%		
...DIO AND TELEVISION														
...amophones, Tape Machines etc.	11,114	10	4	42	8	20	1	*	*	*	6	6	6.0 : 11.0	
...amophone Records	5,788	48	12	27	1	4	3	—	—	—	*	*	8.5 : 5.8	
...dio Receivers	15,391	1	2	69	2	16	*	—	1	*	*	1	12.5 : 15.4	(1)
...levision Receivers	6,418	*	*	53	8	9	26	—	—	—	*	—	2.7 : 6.4	
...SCELLANEOUS MANUFACTURES														
...cuum Flasks	248	21	9	11	4	2	40	—	1	—	*	1	0.3 : 0.2	
...t Manufactures	613	5	7	—	6	13	1	13	—	—	—	—	Neg.: 0.6	
...af Aids	965	13	16	15	—	18	—	—	—	19	13	3	Neg.: 1.0	
...ent Sprays	179	28	3	16	3	—	—	—	—	—	—	—	Neg.: 0.2	
...mbs	227	—	1	96	*	—	—	—	*	—	—	1	0.8 : 0.2	
...ess Buttons	1,479	5	1	41	40	6	—	—	—	*	*	*	1.7 : 1.5	
...okers Pipes	900	2	12	5	32	1	5	—	1	1	—	*	2.3 : 0.9	
...ghters	1,288	3	4	39	*	*	*	—	*	*	7	31	6.0 : 1.3	
...shion Jewellery	3,240	3	5	46	14	*	*	—	—	*	*	21	5.9 : 3.2	
...ncils	1,051	1	2	64	*	1	2	—	—	—	21	3	0.7 : 1.0	
...untain Pens	3,217	15	18	31	24	*	2	—	2	*	4	—	5.0 : 3.2	
...lls	1,832	3	1	10	53	*	*	—	—	—	*	*	1.4 : 1.8	
...ys	8,870	7	22	38	15	3	*	*	*	5	*	*	7.6 : 8.9	
...OD MANUFACTURES														
...scuits and Cakes	9,332	*	4	12	11	35	36	—	—	*	1	*	12.0 : 9.0	
...ms, Jellies, etc.	1,621	*	6	*	*	—	*	—	*	—	*	—	1.0 : 1.6	(2)
...gar Confectionery	3,241	*	6	34	12	11	27	—	—	—	*	*	9.3 : 3.2	
...ocolate Preparations	6,156	—	4	7	11	28	44	—	—	—	3	*	6.6 : 6.1	
...eserved Fruits, other than Dried	11,041	26	*	8	20	19	2	—	—	—	3	—	1.0 : 11.0	
...ups	514	2	7	20	6	*	12	—	—	—	51	—	1.9 : 0.5	
...uces	715	12	31	11	25	—	2	—	—	—	6	—	0.8 : 0.7	
...eese	18,868	—	*	11	22	14	*	*	—	5	39	—	39.4 : 18.9	
...ndensed Milk	231	—	—	—	—	75	—	—	—	25	—	—	18.0 : 0.2	
...ied Fruits	5,582	30	—	—	—	—	—	—	—	—	—	—	0.7 : 5.6	(3)
...rnflakes, Puffed Rice, etc.	407	3	40	—	—	48	—	—	—	6	—	—	Neg.: 0.4	
...OKS AND PRINTED MATTER														
...oks, Brochures and Pamphlets	21,605	5	7	6	20	8	29	—	—	—	25		40.0 : 21.0	
...wspapers, Journals and ...eriodicals	32,628	1	2	4	41	*	49	—	—	—	2	*	24.0 : 32.0	
...TAL IMPORTS ...LL PRODUCTS and ...ERCENTAGE SHARES	$ million 8,722	10	6	18	6	4	6	*	2	*	2	*		

Where a dash is shown imports are nil or negligible.   * Where an asterisk is shown imports are less than 1 per cent.

...otes: Other exporting countries include:

(1) Japan 2%. (2) N. Africa 85%. (3) Spain 9%, Greece 26%, Turkey 13%, Iran 16%, Australia 2%, Jugoslavia 2%.

Product Group and Product	Total Imports $'000	Suppliers' Percentage Share of Imports											Export/ Import Ratio ($ million)	Notes
		U.S.	U.K.	Fr.	It.	Neth.	Bel/ Lux.	Nor.	Swe.	Den.	Switz.	Aust.		
		%	%	%	%	%	%	%	%	%	%	%		
SE METALS														
n and Steel														
ooms & Billets	17,449	—	5	10	—	*	76	*	2	—	—	1	74.0 : 17.0	
n & Steel coils for re-rolling	45,717	—	3	3	—	6	2	—	—	—	—	67	32.0 : 46.0	(1)
n & Steel wire rod	48,713	—	—	40	—	8	34	1	9	—	—	2	49.0 : 48.0	
el Bars	56,574	—	1	22	2	6	55	*	3	1	2	*	103.0 : 57.0	(2)
el Angles, Shapes and Sections	15,561	*	1	34	*	5	44	—	4	2	—	4	45.0 : 15.5	
n & Steel Sheet, heavy	30,785	—	7	15	—	6	25	—	16	2	—	18	113.0 : 31.0	(3)
n & Steel Sheet, medium	17,505	—	5	34	*	6	37	—	—	—	—	6	17.0 : 18.0	(4)
n & Steel Sheet, thin	149,730	—	6	44	3	10	26	1	*	—	—	5	79.0 : 150.0	
Plate	23,859	*	7	47	—	5	38	—	—	—	—	—	22.0 : 24.0	
n & Steel Wire	7,277	*	2	14	*	8	67	—	*	—	*	8	25.0 : 7.3	
dless Tubes and Pipes	15,768	—	1	4	5	22	10	—	47	—	1	1	111.0 : 16.0	
lded Tubes and Pipes	12,420	*	*	26	*	23	32	2	7	*	1	3	88.0 : 12.0	
be & Pipe Fittings	7,581	11	10	14	5	5	3	—	6	*	10	22	34.0 : 7.6	
n-Ferrous Metals														
pper, Bars, Rods, etc.	7,578	1	6	7	*	14	67	—	*	—	2	1	23.8 : 7.6	
pper Plates, Sheets, Strip, etc.	11,738	7	2	9	*	7	45	—	24	—	2	2	11.0 : 11.7	
pper Tubes & Pipes	3,541	*	24	4	*	4	62	—	—	—	1	3	30.5 : 3.5	
ckel Bars, Rods etc.	1,137	31	28	12	—	3	—	—	13	—	11	—	3.1 : 1.1	
ckel Strip, Powders, etc.	624	21	51	10	—	3	2	—	—	—	6	—	5.4 : 0.6	
wrought Aluminium	59,555	15	*	4	—	*	—	24	—	—	14	—	6.9 : 60.0	(5)
minium Bars, Rods, etc.	3,021	5	8	8	6	11	44	—	—	—	15	—	6.1 : 3.0	
minium Plates, Sheet, Strip etc.	12,068	7	6	17	3	21	33	*	1	2	5	2	11.0 : 12.0	
ad, Unwrought	19,517	—	28	18	—	6	8	—	2	—	—	—	5.0 : 19.5	(6)
nc, Unwrought	29,449	—	*	5	—	10	32	7	—	—	—	—	6.3 : 29.5	(7)
n, Unwrought	28,275	—	4	—	—	26	8	—	—	—	—	—	3.2 : 28.3	(8)
gnesium, Unwrought and Wrought	18,550	33	4	—	9	—	—	47	—	—	—	—	Neg : 18.5	
her Non-ferrous metal products	13,183	15	5	3	—	8	27	—	—	—	—	—	5.7 : 13.0	(9)
EMICALS AND CHEMICAL PRODUCTS														
eral and Chemical Fertilizers														
trogenous	3,632	—	—	17	1	*	67	—	—	—	—	—	66.0 : 3.6	
osphatic	6,544	—	—	—	—	7	90	—	—	—	—	—	5.0 : 6.5	(10)
tassic	1,258	—	—	72	19	—	—	—	—	—	—	—	49.0 : 1.2	
ints & Varnishes	8,300	14	10	4	*	46	3	2	4	2	6	6	32.2 : 8.3	
thetic Organic Dyestuffs	17,106	3	11	4	1	3	2	—	—	*	74	—	131.0 : 17.0	
ists Colours	87	10	35	3	10	29	—	—	—	—	—	—	1.4 : 0.1	
ap	871	2	11	60	*	9	3	—	—	3	1	—	2.0 : 0.9	
rfumery & Cosmetics	9,266	9	19	45	2	10	3	—	*	*	8	*	11.3 : 9.2	
lishes, Waxes, etc.	1,039	24	30	4	*	20	1	—	2	2	13	4	3.9 : 1.0	
face-acting Washing preps.	10,206	15	4	14	*	13	35	1	3	*	11	2	34.0 : 10.0	
armaceutical Products														
dicaments	13,116	6	12	13	4	8	4	—	4	6	37	4	116.0 : 13.0	
dding, Gauze, etc.	601	25	2	33	—	29	*	3	—	—	6	—	4.7 : 0.6	
sinfectants, Insecticides, etc.	4,852	23	6	26	5	13	*	—	*	3	21	1	8.0 : 5.0	

Where a dash is shown imports are nil or negligible.   * Where an asterisk is shown imports are less than 1 per cent.

tes: Other exporting countries include:
(1) U.S.S.R. 12%, Japan 3%   (5) Canada 20%, Secret 20%   (8) Malaysia 40%, China 9%
(2) Czechoslovakia 5%.   (6) Mexico 4%, Peru 10%, Australia 15%   (9) U.S.S.R. 13%, China 9%, Japan 6%
(3) Czechoslovakia 6%   (7) U.S.S.R. 5%, Canada 10%, Australia 7%   (10) Poland 3%
(4) Japan 10%   Spain 5%, Congo 6%

Product Group and Product	Total Imports $'000	Suppliers' Percentage Share of Imports											Export/ Import Ratio ($ million)	Note
		U.S.	U.K.	Fr.	It.	Neth.	Bel/ Lux.	Nor.	Swe.	Den.	Switz.	Aust.		
		%	%	%	%	%	%	%	%	%	%	%		
PAPER														
Kraft Paper	66,547	15	—	2	—	1	1	2	44	—	*	2	2.4 : 66.0	(1)
Building Board	9,812	*	*	10	*	11	2	9	43	*	*	2	5.0 : 10.0	(2)
Newsprint	58,426	—	*	*	*	3	*	21	30	—	—	14	0.5 : 59.0	(3)
FACTORY PLANT & EQUIPMENT														
Industrial Machinery														
Steam Boilers	1,495	12	3	15	*	14	16	—	22	9	1	8	37.0 : 1.5	
Aux. Steam Plant	605	41	29	14	—	10	5	—	1	1	*	—	7.1 : 0.6	
Refrigerating Equipment	13,505	23	9	7	19	4	1	2	24	5	2	4	22.8 : 13.5	
Air Conditioning Equipment	2,820	56	4	6	7	9	2	1	6	10	3	—	3.9 : 2.8	
Heating Plant	14,981	21	12	7	12	17	3	*	9	4	10	4	113.0 : 15.0	
Pumping M/c for Liquids	24,039	24	10	12	5	7	2	1	12	7	16	2	82.0 : 24.0	
Pumping M/c for Air and Vacuum	23,875	11	7	4	21	8	7	*	4	11	18	4	27.0 : 24.0	
Centrifugal M/c.	9,101	23	15	6	8	9	2	*	13	3	17	1	59.0 : 9.0	
Production Machinery														
Pulp & Paper Machinery	7,616	11	50	2	1	9	1	*	8	*	12	2	49.7 : 7.6	
Textile Weaving and Knitting Machinery	20,387	4	11	2	4	*	9	—	—	—	67	*	62.8 : 20.0	
Machine Tools for Metal Working	58,731	28	8	8	6	3	6	*	3	*	27	3	367.0 : 59.0	
Rolling Mills Equipment	11,140	36	4	25	1	8	20	—	2	—	*	2	99.0 : 11.0	
Welding Plant	612	9	24	19	—	—	*	—	26	*	9	2	6.1 : 0.6	
Spinning and Doubling M/c.	13,560	9	18	18	9	*	7	—	—	—	33	6	61.5 : 13.5	
Packaging Machinery & Bottling Plant	15,363	22	16	9	11	11	10	*	8	9	*	—	66.7 : 15.3	
Pneumatic M/c. Tools	3,912	35	14	11	—	2	3	—	14	—	2	14	20.5 : 4.0	
Engineering Supplies														
Sandpaper, Emery paper, etc.	1,723	34	1	11	14	3	—	*	5	*	29	—	15.0 : 1.7	
Refractory Goods	867	26	35	10	10	1	*	*	—	—	*	16	7.0 : 0.9	
Fabricated Asbestos	3,183	10	43	26	1	7	4	—	—	3	2	1	3.5 : 3.2	
Ball Bearings	19,351	18	10	15	11	2	*	—	5	*	6	9	47.0 : 19.0	
Rubber Belting	4,583	7	8	44	9	14	2	*	1	2	4	2	7.7 : 4.6	(4)
Textile Belting	298	9	25	4	—	30	12	—	*	—	16	—	0.9 : 0.3	(5)
Transmission Shafts, Gears, etc.	26,885	31	13	11	7	6	7	*	5	2	11	4	85.0 : 27.0	
Taps, Cocks, Valves, etc.	26,520	19	13	9	10	15	4	*	*	6	11	5	78.0 : 26.0	
Metal Bottle Stoppers	4,485	24	3	9	21	17	17	—	—	3	—	2	2.9 : 4.5	
ELECTRICAL PLANT														
Generators, Motors, etc.	38,268	13	7	17	6	11	6	*	3	5	16	8	165.0 : 38.0	
Electrical Circuit Apparatus	41,648	20	6	13	4	16	4	*	2	4	14	6	150.0 : 42.0	
ELECTRICAL EQUIPMENT														
Insulating Cable and Wire	15,774	8	9	28	8	20	5	6	6	*	2	5	50.0 : 16.0	
Insulating Fittings	3,138	9	4	20	3	12	2	—	2	1	28	9	8.5 : 3.0	
Electrical Carbons	1,552	6	10	31	11	1	—	—	—	—	6	—	15.0 : 1.5	
Electric/Electronic Measuring Apparatus	38,155	41	8	6	3	6	13	*	3	2	10	3	78.0 : 38.0	
Electro-Magnets	2,172	28	22	6	7	12	3	—	*	—	7	4	6.6 : 2.0	
Electric Filament Lamps	12,845	13	12	3	—	53	4	—	—	—	1	5	25.0 : 13.0	
Accumulators	4,005	11	1	13	10	11	19	*	8	—	5	16	13.8 : 4.0	
Batteries	2,600	7	38	24	—	5	—	—	—	*	*	2	3.0 : 2.6	(6)
Thermionic Cathode Ray Tubes, Transistors, etc	27,660	31	10	5	10	38	*	—	—	—	3	2	34.0 : 28.0	
Electricity Supply Meters	878	2	—	7	—	3	—	—	—	—	84	—	6.7 : 0.9	

— Where a dash is shown imports are nil or negligible.   * Where an asterisk is shown imports are less than 1 per cent.

Notes: Other exporting countries include:

(1) Finland 33%.   (2) Finland 15%.   (3) Finland 33%.   (4) Japan 20%.   (5) Japan 10%.   (6) Japan 16%.

Product Group and Product	Total Imports $'000	Suppliers' Percentage Share of Imports											Export/Import Ratio ($ million)	Notes
		U.S.	U.K.	Fr.	It.	Neth.	Bel/Lux.	Nor.	Swe.	Den.	Switz.	Aus.		
		%	%	%	%	%	%	%	%	%	%	%		
TRANSPORT EQUIPMENT														
Motor Cars	148,474	3	7	53	27	1	6	—	1	*	—	—	1323 : 149.0	
Automobile Parts and Accessories	45,330	17	11	21	29	5	2	—	1	*	3	3	288.0 : 45.0	
Tractors	26,250	7	60	15	10	3	1	—	2	—	2	*	62.6 : 26.0	
EARTH-MOVING MACHINERY														
Excavating, Levelling, etc. Machinery	64,832	45	20	17	2	2	2	*	2	*	1	5	83.0 : 65.0	
Lifting, Handling Machinery etc.	27,084	15	11	23	2	9	3	4	11	5	4	7	175.0 : 27.0	
AUTOMATIC VENDING EQUIPMENT AND WEIGHING MACHINES														
Automatic Vending Machines	3,075	78	*	*	6	5	4	—	—	3	1	*	4.3 : 3.0	
Weighing Machines	1,403	15	17	4	17	20	7	—	1	3	19	6	21.0 : 1.4	
PHOTOGRAPHIC AND OPTICAL GOODS, SCIENTIFIC INSTRUMENTS AND SUPPLIES														
Cameras	5,529	35	5	6	*	13	*	—	2	—	8	1	56.0 : 5.5	(1)
Lenses, Unmounted and Mounted	3,594	23	12	17	1	8	*	—	—	—	14	*	174.0 : 3.5	
Microscopes	513	17	3	2	*	*	—	—	*	—	22	9	15.0 : 0.5	(2)
Surveying Instruments	3,266	31	27	12	*	3	1	*	3	2	16	1	73.0 : 3.3	
Electro-Medical and X-Ray Apparatus	3,673	17	1	2	6	36	1	—	15	2	6	4	30.0 : 3.7	
Manometers, Thermostats etc.	10,273	31	22	3	3	8	*	—	2	22	4	1	17.7 : 10.3	
Drawing Instruments	6,766	39	4	7	1	2	1	—	5	6	28	2	32.0 : 6.8	
Photographic Chemicals	1,130	32	35	3	*	3	25	—	—	—	—	—	3.5 : 1.1	
Photographic Films	11,529	25	9	21	22	*	22	—	—	—	1	—	21.0 : 11.5	
Photographic Paper	4,685	11	5	7	—	10	64	—	—	—	—	—	23.3 : 4.7	
PLASTICS														
Products of Condensation	27,410	38	7	2	7	12	2	1	5	1	11	1	110.0 : 27.0	
Products of Polymerisation	43,085	24	12	14	21	8	7	*	1	1	4	2	177.0 : 43.0	
Plastic Manufactures	17,382	7	5	12	28	13	3	*	3	4	1	5	46.0 : 17.0	
OFFICE EQUIPMENT														
Typewriters	9,254	32	*	4	19	30	1	—	3	—	3	—	44.0 : 9.0	
Electronic Calculating Machines	8,784	74	15	3	—	4	—	—	*	1	*	—	5.0 : 8.8	
Other Accounting Machines	23,040	19	4	*	39	5	—	1	21	*	5	—	49.0 : 23.0	
Punched Card Machines	39,189	19	18	26	7	3	1	*	17	—	*	—	33.0 : 39.0	
Duplicating Machines	425	7	50	—	6	3	—	—	—	26	2	—	6.9 : 0.4	
TOOLS AND IMPLEMENTS														
Band Saws	3,423	13	2	3	*	2	2	2	17	8	6	1	13.4 : 3.4	(3)
Hand Tools, Pliers, Spanners, Snips, etc.	2,328	21	5	10	1	12	1	—	10	—	8	3	23.3 : 2.3	
Electric Hand Tools	5,111	15	18	5	5	10	3	—	4	*	38	*	21.0 : 5.0	
Other Hand Tools	4,311	17	27	13	3	4	1	—	6	4	16	4	38.0 : 4.3	

Where a dash is shown imports are nil or negligible.   * Where an asterisk is shown imports are less than 1 per cent.

Notes: Other exporting countries include:

(1) Japan 22%.   (2) Japan 40%   (3) Canada 43%.

Product Group and Product	Total Imports ($'000)	Suppliers' Percentage Share of Imports											Export/ Import Ratio ($ million)	Notes
		U.S.	U.K.	Fr.	It.	Neth.	Bel/ Lux.	Nor.	Swe.	Den.	Switz.	Aus.		
		%	%	%	%	%	%	%	%	%	%	%		
TEXTILES AND CLOTHING														
Woven & Knitted Fabrics														
Woollen Fabrics	112,780	*	14	14	49	9	7	*	*	*	4	1	22.0 : 113.0	
Cotton Fabrics, bleached and unbleached	62,335	1	2	21	5	25	9	—	2	*	14	6	82.0 : 62.0	
Linen Fabrics	1,285	*	15	1	4	3	30	—	3	4	17	2	1.0 : 1.3	
Fabrics of Man-made Fibres, (Synthetic and Artificial)	73,380	3	4	12	26	11	15	—	*	*	10	7	102.0 : 73.0	
Knitted Fabrics	30,803	4	1	13	12	47	4	—	2	*	8	3	34.0 : 31.0	
Narrow Fabrics	2,689	6	9	17	1	12	10	—	1	*	8	4	6.7 : 2.7	(1)
Clothing														
Leather Footwear	67,794	*	2	12	54	4	1	*	*	—	6	1	23.0 : 68.0	
Knitted Outerwear	78,107	*	3	19	37	4	3	*	*	*	2	5	19.0 : 78.0	(2)
Knitted Underwear	13,413	1	2	10	55	8	3	*	2	*	8	1	10.0 : 13.0	
Mens Underwear	16,370	*	*	5	3	4	3	—	1	—	*	1	1.5 : 16.4	(3)
Mens Outerwear	39,857	5	2	5	14	13	8	*	1	2	2	21	28.0 : 40.0	(4)
Womens Outerwear	44,747	1	3	15	22	13	6	—	1	*	6	7	13.0 : 45.0	(5)
Womens Underwear	5,532	2	*	21	6	9	5	—	—	—	9	14	0.7 : 5.5	(6)
Stockings	8,962	8	2	23	35	7	3	3	—	*	4	10	11.6 : 9.0	
Corsetry	5,706	9	4	18	*	16	1	—	4	*	2	25	10.1 : 5.7	
HOUSEHOLD AND CONSUMER DURABLES														
Domestic Refrigerators	3,177	8	5	8	54	—	4	—	9	1	1	10	26.0 : 3.0	
Domestic Washing Machines	7,240	9	49	17	18	1	2	—	—	—	*	—	42.0 : 7.0	
Electric Domestic Appliances	8,207	2	41	15	6	15	7	*	*	1	10	—	19.0 : 8.0	
Carpets	40,499	*	7	2	6	15	55	—	*	5	*	1	8.6 : 40.5	
Linoleum	14,036	—	2	87	—	*	10	—	—	—	*	—	7.8 : 14.0	
Sewing Machines	16,934	23	9	2	14	7	2	—	2	*	9	4	59.0 : 17.0	
Household Glassware	8,734	2	4	23	15	4	13	*	9	2	2	6	18.0 : 8.7	
Household Chinaware	2,159	—	4	6	1	1	10	—	3	8	*	*	34.0 : 2.0	(7)
Bed and Table Linen	9,769	2	4	10	11	11	16	*	1	2	7	3	7.5 : 9.8	
Electric Razors	2,221	14	11	28	9	11	—	—	—	*	25	—	7.4 : 2.2	
Spoons and Forks	3,156	—	12	9	2	3	—	1	2	1	2	5	8.3 : 3.2	
Knives	1,344	—	7	3	23	4	—	—	1	1	6	2	9.8 : 1.3	
Scissors	360	—	4	—	65	20	—	—	—	—	—	—	7.9 : 0.4	
Aluminium Domestic Utensils	577	1	7	23	25	6	5	7	4	2	15	3	3.5 : 0.6	
Brushware	1,546	7	7	29	4	6	9	11	3	3	8	3	9.5 : 1.5	
WATCHES AND CLOCKS														
Watches	12,099	1	—	2	—	1	—	—	—	—	94	—	15.0 : 12.0	
Clocks	963	18	16	7	6	11	—	—	—	—	36	4	34.0 : 1.0	
MISCELLANEOUS METAL MANUFACTURES														
Locks, etc.	1,677	20	3	26	36	5	6	—	6	2	8	—	15.0 : 1.7	
Safes, etc.	449	—	—	5	—	15	—	7	—	73	—	—	0.8 : 0.5	
Iron and Steel Chain	2,027	23	27	6	11	15	5	—	3	2	5	—	21.0 : 2.0	
Iron and Steel Springs	2,908	17	18	5	16	2	2	—	2	1	20	13	10.0 : 3.0	
RUBBER MANUFACTURES														
Tyres	49,130	3	6	20	6	11	13	6	10	—	7	11	49.0 : 49.0	
General Rubber Manufactures	10,274	50	9	9	11	5	—	—	3	3	4	1	13.0 : 10.0	

— Where a dash is shown imports are nil or negligible.   * Where an asterisk is shown imports are less than 1 per cent.

Notes: Other exporting countries include:

(1) Japan 28%.   (3) Hong Kong 71%.   (5) Hong Kong 12%.   (7) Japan 60%.
(2) Hong Kong 15%.   (4) Hong Kong 10%.   (6) Hong Kong 29%.

Product Group and Product	Total Imports $'000	Suppliers' Percentage Share of Imports											Export/ Import Ratio ($ million)	Notes
		U.S.	U.K.	Fr.	It.	Neth.	Bel/ Lux.	Nor.	Swe.	Den.	Switz.	Aus.		
		%	%	%	%	%	%	%	%	%	%	%		
IO AND TELEVISION														
nophones, Tape Machines														
.c.	10,002	36	6	4	4	20	*	*	—	*	5	13	41.0 : 10.0	
nophone Records	6,042	23	23	9	3	26	4	—	*	*	6	3	19.5 : 6.0	
io Receivers	10,189	1	1	2	5	17	*	—	*	*	*	5	69.0 : 6.0	(1)
vision Receivers	3,248	*	8	*	18	6	40	—	—	—	16	—	43.0 : 3.0	
CELLANEOUS														
ANUFACTURES														
um Flasks	137	2	5	2	6	5	—	—	18	—	4	—	1.0 : Neg.	
Manufactures	726	2	8	13	12	8	6	—	—	—	—	—	0.7 : 0.7	
Aids	709	16	4	—	—	27	—	—	*	27	14	10	1.6 : 0.7	
t Sprays	335	9	1	81	*	—	—	—	—	—	—	—	1.6 : 0.3	
bs	188	*	4	27	11	3	6	—	—	—	2	45	2.7 : 0.2	
s Buttons	3,214	2	1	`14	54	8	2	—	*	1	1	5	9.3 : 3.2	
kers Pipes	979	7	19	20	25	2	3	—	—	6	—	4	0.6 : 1.0	
ters	2,576	4	1	47	*	1	*	—	*	*	10	12	5.0 : 2.5	
tion Jewellery	1,219	2	7	7	7	3	1	—	—	2	2	21	5.0 : 1.2	(2)
cils	261	10	2	10	3	6	*	—	1	—	—	19	8.5 : 0.3	(3)
tain Pens	1,833	10	3	13	12	3	*	—	4	2	32	3	17.6 : 1.8	(4)
s	2,692	4	*	5	76	3	*	—	—	—	*	*	1.9 : 2.7	
s	12,762	3	20	7	10	8	1	*	*	20	*	3	31.0 : 13.0	(5)
D MANUFACTURES														
uits and Cakes	12,922	*	*	17	3	56	11	*	—	7	5	*	2.7 : 13.0	
s, Jellies, etc.	1,179	*	23	15	*	*	12	—	4	—	2	—	0.2 : 1.2	
r Confectionery	10,888	*	20	12	5	39	11	—	*	*	2	1	3.6 : 11.0	
colate Preparations	20,397	2	12	14	2	28	12	—	3	—	21	1	5.4 : 21.0	
erved Fruits, other than														
ied	47,779	38	*	*	4	4	1	—	—	—	*	—	0.5 : 48.0	(6)
s	414	1	14	3	9	13	53	—	—	—	7	—	1.4 : 0.4	
es	1,420	14	29	1	22	24	1	—	—	—	*	—	0.9 : 1.4	
se	77,792	—	*	11	1	38	2	2	1	28	4	*	16.0 : 78.0	
densed Milk	2,143	—	—	90	—	9	—	—	—	1	—	—	0.2 : 2.1	
d Fruits	17,237	10	—	3	—	—	—	—	—	—	—	—	0.3 : 17.0	(7)
flakes, Puffed Rice, etc.	1,101	—	77	—	—	—	—	—	—	22	—	—	Neg. : 1.0	
KS AND PRINTED														
ATTER														
ks, Brochures and														
amphlets	17,010	5	5	4	5	8	2	—	—	*	26	36	38.0 : 17.0	
spapers, Journals and														
eriodicals	3,416	6	9	15	16	20	1	—	—	—	24	6	24.2 : 3.4	
AL IMPORTS	$ million													
PRODUCTS and														
ERCENTAGE SHARES	12,994	15	5	10	7	9	6	1	4	2	3	2		

here a dash is shown imports are nil or negligible.   * Where an asterisk is shown imports are less than 1 per cent.

es: Other exporting countries include:

(1) Japan 65%.   (4) Japan 18%.   (7) Spain 1%, Greece 36%, Turkey 12%, Iran 20%,
(2) Japan 25%   (5) Japan, Hong Kong, 30%.   Australia 7%, Jugoslavia 3%.
(3) Israel 25%, Japan 23%. (6) Spain, China, Formosa, etc. 58%.

Product Group and Product	Total Imports $'000	Suppliers' Percentage Share of Imports											Export/ Import Ratio ($ million)	Notes
		U.S.	U.K.	Fr.	Ger.	Neth.	Bel/Lux.	Nor.	Swe.	Den.	Switz.	Aust.		
		%	%	%	%	%	%	%	%	%	%	%		
E METALS														
and Steel														
ms & Billets	34,145	*	*	13	33	*	13	*	1	–	–	–	0.4 : 34.0	(1)
& Steel coils for -rolling	89,417	–	4	11	21	4	9	*	–	–	–	4	1.8 : 89.0	(2)
& Steel wire rod	17,656	–	–	35	26	*	11	–	10	–	–	7	1.4 : 17.6	(3)
Bars	12,448	–	2	16	51	*	10	–	–	–	–	7	6.0 : 12.0	
Angles, Shapes and ctions	29,943	–	4	8	50	–	22	–	–	–	2	–	2.5 : 30.0	
& Steel Sheet, heavy	46,155	–	5	6	45	8	5	–	6	–	–	1	6.0 : 46.0	(4)
& Steel Sheet, medium	8,594	–	3	18	39	8	11	–	–	–	–	–	2.2 : 8.6	(5)
& Steel Sheet, thin	72,730	–	*	35	18	4	16	–	–	–	–	2	24.0 : 73.0	(6)
Plate	26,079	11	26	22	7	20	11	–	–	–	–	–	9.0 : 26.0	
& Steel Wire	5,316	*	2	3	18	2	28	–	15	–	4	18	1.5 : 5.3	(7)
less Tubes and Pipes	10,810	–	21	4	38	1	1	–	20	–	*	3	21.0 : 11.0	
ed Tubes and Pipes	5,145	13	5	9	46	5	2	2	5	–	3	3	42.0 : 5.0	
& Pipe Fittings	11,959	8	9	10	33	*	*	2	2	–	3	6	5.5 : 12.0	(8)
Ferrous Metals														
er Bars, Rods, etc.	4,783	2	8	9	12	*	2	–	*	–	21	1	1.8 : 4.8	(9)
er Plates, Sheets, Strip, c.	3,514	15	9	10	23	3	1	–	14	–	2	–	4.6 : 3.5	(10)
er Tubes & Pipes	2,686	*	33	*	26	–	*	–	–	–	2	14	2.6 : 2.7	
el Bars, Rods etc.	1,478	15	30	10	20	1	–	–	10	–	7	–	0.1 : 1.5	
el Strip, Powders, etc.	1,392	20	36	–	30	–	*	–	–	–	6	–	1.0 : 1.4	
rought Aluminium	24,348	25	–	5	1	–	1	19	–	–	2	11	0.1 : 24.0	(11)
inium Bars, Rods, etc.	2,091	10	1	2	15	–	46	14	–	–	10	–	1.0 : 2.1	(12)
inium Plates, Sheet, Strip c.	11,516	5	3	28	24	5	1	–	–	–	9	1	4.7 : 11.5	
, Unwrought	6.700	*	*	*	*	–	1	–	–	–	–	5	Neg. : 6.7	(13)
, Unwrought	6,659	–	2	4	2	8	11	–	–	–	–	7	Neg. : 6.7	(14)
Unwrought	10,247	*	1	–	–	4	2	–	–	–	–	–	Neg. : 10.3	(15)
esium, Unwrought and ought	91	43	16	–	–	–	–	–	–	–	–	–	– –	
r Non-ferrous metal oducts	2,926	13	13	3	1	4	41	–	–	–	–	–	Neg. : 3.0	
MICALS AND CHEMICAL RODUCTS														
ral and Chemical ertilizers														
genous	293	–	–	–	–	–	–	–	–	–	–	–	48.0 : 0.3	
sphatic	488	–	–	–	19	15	42	–	–	–	–	–	1.4 : 0.5	
ssic	5,033	–	–	16	13	–	–	–	–	–	–	–	3.3 : 5.0	(16)
ts & Varnishes	5,868	28	12	10	31	4	6	*	*	*	2	–	3.6 : 5.9	
hetic Organic Dyestuffs	25,469	4	9	7	44	2	*	–	–	*	32	–	5.0 : 26.0	
sts Colours	355	*	23	5	44	22	–	–	–	–	–	–	Neg. : 0.4	
	760	8	7	33	10	35	*	–	–	–	2	–	0.9 : 0.8	
umery & Cosmetics	5,647	5	16	44	15	4	*	–	1	–	12	*	2.0 : 5.6	
shes, Waxes, etc.	841	5	49	5	33	2	*	–	1	–	3	–	0.1 : 1.0	
ace-acting Washing preps.	9,171	15	9	5	44	2	5	–	*	–	11	5	2.4 : 9.1	
rmaceutical Products														
icaments	23,926	16	5	5	28	9	*	–	2	1	30	*	25.0 : 24.0	
ding, Gauze, etc.	753	15	14	20	28	11	5	–	2	–	2	–	0.3 : 0.8	
nfectants, Insecticides, c.	5,211	18	3	8	53	6	*	–	–	–	3	5	8.0 : 5.0	

here a dash is shown imports are nil or negligible.   * Where an asterisk is shown imports are less than 1 per cent.

es: Other exporting countries include:

(1) U.S.S.R., Hungary, Rumania 30%.   (6) Japan 8%.   (11) U.S.S.R. 5%, Canada 20%.
(2) U.S.S.R. 10%, Canada 7%, Japan 23%.   (7) Jugoslavia 13%. (12) Canada 20%.
(3) Jugoslavia 10%.   (8) Japan 20%.   (13) Mexico, Peru, 42%, Australia 30%, Jugoslavia 8%, U.S.S.R. 6%.
(4) Japan 8%.   (9) Jugoslavia 25%. (14) Jugoslavia 15%, African Territories 15%, Mexico, Peru 15%, Australia 20%.
(5) Japan 16%.   (10) Jugoslavia 37%. (15) Malaysia 85%. (16) U.S.S.R. 20%, Israel 30%.

Product Group and Product	Total Imports $'000	Suppliers' Percentage Share of Imports											Export/ Import Ratio ($ million)	Note
		U.S.	U.K.	Fr.	Ger.	Neth.	Bel/ Lux.	Nor.	Swe.	Den.	Switz.	Aust.		
		%	%	%	%	%	%	%	%	%	%	%		
PAPER														
Kraft Paper	29,263	19	—	*	*	*	*	*	32	—	—	3	0.3 : 29.3	(1)
Building Board	2,131	*	—	8	1	—	14	—	1	—	3	67	1.8 : 2.0	
Newsprint	779	2	—	—	*	—	—	10	19	—	—	4	0.3 : 0.8	(2)
FACTORY PLANT & EQUIPMENT														
Industrial Machinery														
Steam Boilers	3,868	16	3	*	47	1	2	—	6	*	5	16	7.1 : 3.9	(3)
Aux. Steam Plant	2,303	20	11	*	57	2	1	—	1	—	4	3	0.8 : 2.3	
Refrigerating Equipment	3,112	37	7	11	24	2	*	*	10	5	2	—	15.0 : 3.0	
Air Conditioning Equipment	2,637	77	9	4	6	1	—	—	1	—	1	—	1.2 : 2.6	
Heating Plant	23,090	18	10	11	43	2	2	—	4	4	5	*	48.0 : 23.0	
Pumping M/c for Liquids	21,386	16	13	14	45	1	*	*	2	*	5	1	18.0 : 21.0	
Pumping M/c for Air and Vacuum	27,355	21	9	9	35	1	4	—	5	2	6	5	13.0 : 27.0	(4)
Centrifugal M/c.	14,600	21	7	9	40	5	1	*	7	*	7	*	6.3 : 14.6	
Production Machinery														
Pulp & Paper Machinery	13,592	14	21	7	30	5	*	*	5	—	4	2	6.2 : 13.6	
Textile Weaving and Knitting Machinery	24,978	3	20	4	28	*	10	—	*	*	31	—	18.0 : 25.0	
Machine Tools for Metal Working	110,159	28	7	6	40	1	2	*	1	*	8	*	62.0 : 110.0	
Rolling Mills Equipment	20,887	64	11	4	14	—	3	—	1	—	*	*	5.6 : 21.0	
Welding Plant	2,209	63	1	6	23	—	*	—	1	1	*	3	0.1 : 2.2	
Spinning and Doubling M/c.	18,746	3	13	15	39	—	11	—	—	—	15	—	26.0 : 19.0	
Packaging Machinery & Bottling Plant	13,646	12	6	6	52	3	8	—	6	4	*	—	11.0 : 13.6	
Pneumatic M/c. Tools	5,717	17	8	9	10	1	7	—	25	—	1	7	0.6 : 5.7	
Engineering Supplies														
Sandpaper, Emery paper, etc.	5,635	16	2	5	66	—	*	—	1	*	9	—	1.1 : 5.6	
Refractory Goods	1,380	11	27	14	41	1	*	*	—	—	*	4	0.4 : 1.4	
Fabricated Asbestos	2,173	9	39	12	24	1	1	—	—	—	1	12	0.7 : 2.2	
Ball Bearings	13,280	17	7	5	41	1	*	—	22	*	4	3	16.0 : 13.0	
Rubber Belting	1,897	10	20	22	25	3	1	*	3	12	2	2	1.4 : 1.9	
Textile Belting	208	9	29	20	33	—	—	—	3	—	6	—	Neg.: 0.2	
Transmission Shafts, Gears, etc.	24,984	16	18	8	44	1	2	*	3	1	5	1	8.0 : 25.0	
Taps, Cocks, Valves, etc.	24,551	29	14	6	40	2	*	*	1	2	2	*	30.0 : 24.0	
Metal Bottle Stoppers	1,182	2	31	5	4	34	—	—	—	*	—	2	1.7 : 1.2	
ELECTRICAL PLANT														
Generators, Motors, etc.	44,926	25	4	12	41	2	4	*	3	*	3	2	41.0 : 45.0	
Electrical Circuit Apparatus	48,303	31	6	12	34	4	*	*	*	*	5	1	33.0 : 48.0	
ELECTRICAL EQUIPMENT														
Insulating Cable and Wire	4,897	24	5	16	41	4	1	—	1	—	4	—	11.0 : 5.0	
Insulating Fittings	3,278	13	3	20	27	—	12	—	—	—	19	2	1.2 : 3.3	
Electrical Carbons	6,472	5	7	14	53	—	—	—	—	—	6	—	5.0 : 6.5	
Electric/Electronic Measuring Apparatus	29,683	46	11	4	22	3	*	*	1	*	6	1	8.3 : 30.0	
Electro-Magnets	2,972	38	12	15	24	5	—	—	*	—	1	3	0.5 : 3.0	
Electric Filament Lamps	6,824	14	6	6	31	38	1	—	—	—	1	*	2.7 : 6.8	
Accumulators	1,753	18	12	6	46	2	—	—	7	—	1	5	0.9 : 1.7	
Batteries	2,106	9	14	22	8	—	—	—	—	4	—	—	Neg.: 2.0	(5)
Thermionic Cathode Ray Tubes, Transistors, etc	25,340	34	6	9	13	34	*	—	—	—	2	*	10.0 : 25.0	
Electricity Supply Meters	1,541	*	—	1	22	—	—	—	—	—	76	—	0.1 : 1.5	

— Where a dash is shown imports are nil or negligible.   * Where an asterisk is shown imports are less than 1 per cent.

Notes: Other exporting countries include:

(1) Finland 38%.   (2) Finland 46%.   (3) Canada 4%.   (4) U.S.S.R. 1%.   (5) Japan 27%.

Product Group and Product	Total Imports ($'000)	Suppliers' Percentage Share of Imports											Export/ Import Ratio ($ million)	Notes
		U.S.	U.K.	Fr.	Ger.	Neth.	Bel/ Lux.	Nor.	Swe.	Den.	Switz.	Aus.		
		%	%	%	%	%	%	%	%	%	%	%		
XTILES AND CLOTHING														
ven & Knitted Fabrics														
ollen Fabrics	19,092	*	60	22	3	*	2	—	*	*	5	4	141.0 : 19.0	
tton Fabrics, bleached and unbleached	29,372	5	6	20	14	4	6	—	—	*	9	1	22.6 : 29.4	(1)
en Fabrics	3,113	*	32	37	2	1	14	—	*	*	2	*	0.3 : 3.0	
rics of Man-made Fibres, (Synthetic and Artificial)	13,341	4	1	12	42	4	1	—	*	*	12	4	87.0 : 13.0	
tted Fabrics	3,299	6	3	10	66	5	1	—	*	—	5	*	10.7 : 3.3	
rrow Fabrics	2,336	19	5	12	55	*	*	—	—	*	6	1	1.0 : 2.4	
thing														
ather Footwear	846	4	21	21	7	1	*	—	—	—	14	—	162.0 : 0.9	(2)
tted Outerwear	6,037	*	62	17	4	*	*	2	2	—	2	6	184.0 : 6.0	
tted Underwear	1,698	*	10	18	26	—	—	1	*	—	40	4	2.4 : 1.7	
s Underwear	297	5	6	55	1	*	—	—	—	—	—	—	6.7 : 0.3	
s Outerwear	2,520	3	31	12	25	3	*	*	*	*	2	3	22.0 : 2.5	(3)
mens Outerwear	2,566	2	20	32	20	8	1	—	—	—	2	6	33.0 : 2.6	
mens Underwear	103	22	14	18	26	8	—	—	—	—	10	2	1.8 : 0.1	
ckings	1,001	7	13	8	56	—	—	11	—	—	*	—	32.0 : 1.0	
rsetry	3,912	6	9	12	44	1	*	—	—	*	2	22	0.3 : 3.9	
USEHOLD AND CONSUMER DURABLES														
mestic Refrigerators	2,427	3	4	5	86	—	*	—	2	—	*	1	35.0 : 2.4	
mestic Washing Machines	9,947	3	45	5	45	*	*	—	—	—	*	—	10.6 : 10.0	
ctric Domestic Appliances	4,285	2	21	45	23	3	*	*	*	*	*	1	3.5 : 4.3	
rpets	1,898	2	11	7	27	6	12	—	—	1	1	2	9.3 : 2.0	
noleum	541	—	—	45	24	—	1	—	—	—	23	4	Neg.: 0.5	
wing Machines	9,853	17	9	2	64	*	*	—	*	*	5	—	17.4 : 10.0	
usehold Glassware	7,998	*	*	31	26	*	5	—	2	*	*	1	12.9 : 8.0	
usehold Chinaware	12,031	*	1	4	72	*	*	—	*	*	*	*	0.5 : 12.0	(4)
d and Table Linen	6,032	10	2	8	10	*	1	*	*	*	2	—	3.5 : 6.0	
ectric Razors	2,938	9	1	6	25	48	—	—	—	*	4	5	0.7 : 2.9	
ons and Forks	619	3	8	11	61	*	1	1	*	1	*	10	0.9 : 0.6	
ives	488	3	16	16	37	—	—	—	*	*	15	7	1.4 : 0.5	
ssors	169	—	*	5	91	—	—	—	—	—	—	—	3.2 : 0.2	
miniunm Domestic Utensils	285	1	62	15	12	—	—	—	—	—	2	5	4.6 : 0.3	
shware	854	4	16	8	56	2	*	—	2	*	4	1	0.7 : 0.9	
TCHES AND CLOCKS														
tches	15,814	1	*	1	*	—	*	—	—	—	97	—	0.4 : 16.0	
cks	4,310	*	1	6	80	1	—	—	—	—	9	—	0.4 : 4.3	
SCELLANEOUS METAL MANUFACTURES														
cks, etc.	1,220	5	12	21	56	*	—	—	1	—	3	—	5.2 : 1.2	
es, etc.	115	2	*	—	80	10	—	—	—	—	—	—	Neg.: 0.1	
n and Steel Chain	2,194	14	22	3	47	5	*	—	1	2	3	3	1.6 : 2.2	
n and Steel Springs	1,283	11	12	28	27	*	1	—	*	—	20	1	0.9 : 1.3	
BBER MANUFACTURES														
res	10,194	3	11	38	wr	1	7	—	*	—	7	6	34.0 : 10.0	
neral Rubber Manufactures	3,524	14	27	6	34	3	*	—	1	*	2	2	3.4 : 3.5	

Where a dash is shown imports are nil or negligible.   * Where an asterisk is shown imports are less than 1 per cent.

tes: Other exporting countries include:

    (1) India, China, Hong Kong, Formosa, Egypt, etc. 30%.   (3) Hong Kong 10%.
    (2) Japan, Hong Kong, etc. 20%.   (4) Japan 9%.

Product Group and Product	Total Imports $'000	Suppliers' Percentage Share of Imports											Export/ Import Ratio ($ million)	Note
		U.S.	U.K.	Fr.	Ger.	Neth.	Bel/ Lux.	Nor.	Swe.	Den.	Switz.	Aus.		
		%	%	%	%	%	%	%	%	%	%	%		
TRANSPORT EQUIPMENT														
Motor Cars	198,031	1	14	31	53	*	1	—	*	—	—	—	249.0 : 198.0	
Automobile Parts and Accessories	61,256	2	33	40	24	*	*	—	*	—	*	1	52.0 : 61.0	
Tractors	16,093	14	45	8	24	—	*	—	—	—	1	4	37.2 : 16.0	
EARTH-MOVING MACHINERY														
Excavating, Levelling, etc. Machinery	28,670	41	25	12	10	*	1	*	2	*	*	*	18.5 : 29.0	(1)
Lifting, Handling Machinery etc.	45,107	31	8	10	40	2	1	1	2	1	2	*	21.0 : 45.0	
AUTOMATIC VENDING EQUIPMENT AND WEIGHING MACHINES														
Automatic Vending Machines	611	38	8	1	38	—	3	—	—	8	2	—	0.3 : 0.6	
Weighing Machines	3,465	13	1	4	64	6	4	—	*	*	5	1	1.7 : 3.5	
PHOTOGRAPHIC AND OPTICAL GOODS, SCIENTIFIC INSTRU-MENTS AND SUPPLIES														
Cameras	5,196	8	10	1	63	1	*	—	1	—	*	1	0.6 : 5.2	(2)
Lenses, Unmounted and Mounted	2,174	3	5	14	50	*	*	—	1	—	12	*	0.4 : 2.2	
Microscopes	1,125	4	3	1	60	—	—	—	*	—	8	15	0.1 : 1.1	
Surveying Instruments	20,163	14	2	*	76	2	*	*	*	*	3	*	15.0 : 20.0	
Electro-Medical and X-Ray Apparatus	3,603	16	4	7	41	15	*	—	6	1	4	2	3.0 : 3.6	
Manometers, Thermostats etc.	10,481	33	15	12	21	6	*	—	*	2	5	2	3.6 : 10.5	
Drawing Instruments	5,558	16	10	11	41	*	*	—	2	*	1	*	3.5 : 5.5	
Photographic Chemicals	1,140	27	12	5	31	2	22	—	—	—	—	—	0.2 : 1.1	
Photographic Films	9,678	17	2	47	18	—	15	—	—	—	*	—	7.3 : 9.7	
Photographic Paper	4,746	10	10	14	43	6	16	—	—	—	—	—	0.7 : 4.8	
PLASTICS														
Products of Condensation	21,860	19	7	8	49	5	1	*	2	*	6	*	10.0 : 22.0	
Products of Polymerisation	23,990	19	9	9	46	5	5	—	*	*	*	1	61.0 : 24.0	
Plastic Manufactures	9,749	13	5	13	47	3	2	*	6	1	5	*	20.0 : 10.0	
OFFICE EQUIPMENT														
Typewriters	4,201	40	1	11	23	9	—	—	13	—	2	—	25.0 : 4.0	
Electronic Calculating Machines	355	4	66	12	12	—	—	—	—	—	—	—	0.3 : 0.4	
Other Accounting Machines	6,763	14	8	1	38	3	—	*	19	*	4	*	75.0 : 6.8	
Punched Card Machines	18,606	24	9	27	25	3	*	*	5	*	*	*	9.4 : 18.6	
Duplicating Machines	462	3	38	—	33	*	—	—	*	21	2	—	0.5 : 0.5	
TOOLS AND IMPLEMENTS														
Hand Saws	3,911	17	5	3	48	*	2	*	16	*	3	4	0.4 : 3.9	(3)
Hand Tools, Pliers, Spanners, Snips, etc.	4,171	9	4	4	57	12	*	—	4	—	4	2	1.5 : 4.2	
Electric Hand Tools	3,090	6	6	6	68	1	1	—	*	*	11	—	1.5 : 3.0	
Other Hand Tools	3,487	4	5	8	70	*	1	—	4	*	3	2	2.0 : 3.5	

— Where a dash is shown imports are nil or negligible.   * Where an asterisk is shown imports are less than 1 per cent.

Notes: Other exporting countries include:
(1) Japan 3%.   (2) Japan 11%.   (3) Canada 3%.

Product Group and Product	Total Imports $'000	Suppliers' Percentage Share of Imports											Export/ Import Ratio ($ million)	Notes
		U.S.	U.K.	Fr.	Ger.	Neth.	Bel/ Lux.	Nor.	Swe.	Den.	Switz.	Aus.		
		%	%	%	%	%	%	%	%	%	%	%		
DIO AND TELEVISION														
mophones, Tape Machines, tc.	7,103	24	7	7	25	26	–	–	–	–	1	2	3.5 : 7.0	
mophone Records	3,543	41	18	8	24	5	*	–	–	–	1	*	1.7 : 3.5	
io Receivers	3,123	5	2	2	60	13	*	–	*	*	*	–	3.3 : 3.1	(1)
evision Receivers	4,732	3	–	–	66	18	7	–	–	1	*	–	1.8 : 4.7	
CELLANEOUS MANUFACTURES														
uum Flasks	417	3	8	6	40	–	–	–	–	–	*	1	Neg. : 0.4	
Manufactures	154	2	8	6	67	–	1	2	–	–	–	–	0.1 : 0.2	
f Aids	790	24	7	–	8	4	–	–	–	43	9	4	1.0 : 0.8	
nt Sprays	193	9	3	59	23	–	–	–	–	–	–	2	Neg. : 0.2	
nbs	238	2	5	5	35	–	–	–	–	–	2	50	0.2 : 0.2	
ss Buttons	863	7	7	15	58	1	–	–	–	*	*	2	7.1 : 0.9	
kers Pipes	189	2	20	32	11	5	1	–	–	*	–	10	4.5 : 0.2	
hters	1,209	*	33	40	13	2	–	–	–	–	9	1	Neg. : 1.2	
hion Jewellery	1,520	5	*	7	31	2	*	*	–	–	*	33	Neg. : 1.5	
cils	890	2	1	4	71	2	–	–	–	–	3	10	Neg. : 0.9	
ntain Pens	2,444	9	8	17	55	*	*	–	3	*	5	–	7.5 : 2.4	
ls	276	15	*	19	29	2	–	–	–	–	*	–	7.0 : 0.3	
s	7,915	4	12	10	28	*	*	*	*	5	*	*	8.1 : 8.0	
OD MANUFACTURES														
cuits and Cakes	2,177	–	10	61	7	8	*	5	–	*	8	*	2.7 : 2.1	
ns; Jellies, etc.	392	*	14	5	7	2	–	–	–	–	6	–	0.2 : 0.4	(2)
ar Confectionery	1,569	5	22	14	5	24	1	–	–	2	6	4	3.7 : 1.6	
ocolate Preparations	981	–	5	8	23	18	2	–	–	–	39	3	4.7 : 1.0	
served Fruits, other than Dried	1,672	47	*	*	1	–	–	–	–	–	–	–	7.2 : 1.7	(3)
ps	871	*	6	12	*	3	–	–	–	–	77	–	1.0 : 0.9	
ces	589	5	14	*	77	–	*	–	–	–	*	–	0.8 : 0.6	
ese	50,792	–	–	12	20	2	*	3	3	8	26	13	31.3 : 51.0	
ndensed Milk	622	20	–	15	–	6	38	–	–	6	–	–	0.1 : 0.6	
ed Fruits	5,131	34	–	–	–	–	–	–	–	–	–	–	1.2 : 5.1	(4)
nflakes, Puffed Rice, etc.	103	15	78	–	–	–	–	–	–	3	–	–	Neg : 0.1	
OKS AND PRINTED MATTER														
ks, Brochures and Pamphlets	6,023	48	7	16	10	3	1	–	–	4	6	6	10.0 : 6.0	
wspapers, Journals and Periodicals	2,660	12	14	18	43	1	*	–	–	–	2	2	19.0 : 2.6	
TAL IMPORTS L PRODUCTS and PERCENTAGE SHARES	$ million 7,538	14	6	10	17	3	3	*	2	1	3	3		

Where a dash is shown imports are nil or negligible.   * Where an asterisk is shown imports are less than 1 per cent.

tes: Other exporting countries include:

(1) Japan 12%.   (2) Australia 25%.   (3) Spain, S. Africa, etc. 45%.   (4) Greece 20%, Turkey 40%, Jugoslavia 7%.

Product Group and Product	Total Imports $'000	Suppliers' Percentage Share of Imports											Export/ Import Ratio ($ million)	Notes
		U.S.	U.K.	Fr.	Ger.	It.	Bel/ Lux.	Nor.	Swe.	Den.	Switz.	Aust.		
		%	%	%	%	%	%	%	%	%	%	%		
ASE METALS														
n and Steel														
ooms & Billets	6,689	—	*	8	25	—	—	66	—	—	—	—	2.2 : 7.0	
n & Steel coils for re-rolling	14,078	—	13	—	*	—	1	—	—	—	—	—	36.0 : 14.0	(1)
n & Steel wire rod	9,183	—	—	24	34	—	38	—	—	—	—	—	8.0 : 9.0	(2)
el Bars	45,326	—	1	5	31	—	56	—	—	—	—	1	3.0 : 45.0	(3)
el Angles, Shapes and Sections	54,803	—	4	4	51	—	37	—	—	—	—	—	5.0 : 55.0	
n & Steel Sheet, heavy	18,674	—	1	2	68	—	14	—	1	*	—	3	16.0 : 19.0	(4)
n & Steel Sheet, medium	3,444	—	—	2	54	—	38	—	—	—	—	*	2.5 : 3.4	
n & Steel Sheet, thin	17,660	—	9	12	28	—	38	*	2	—	—	8	70.0 : 17.6	
n Plate	8,168	3	8	7	27	—	52	—	—	—	—	—	19.0 : 8.0	
n & Steel Wire	6,270	*	3	*	22	*	73	—	*	—	*	—	3.3 : 6.3	
Idless Tubes and Pipes	22,898	—	11	3	59	2	5	—	13	—	*	—	6.8 : 23.0	
lded Tubes and Pipes	14,751	10	16	7	42	—	26	—	2	—	1	1	14.0 : 15.0	
be & Pipe Fittings	7,878	7	12	3	56	1	11	—	2	*	7	*	2.3 : 7.9	
n-Ferrous Metals														
pper Bars, Rods, etc.	13,691	*	9	1	22	—	61	*	4	—	—	*	3.2 : 13.7	
pper Plates, Sheets, Strip, etc.	9,839	*	6	3	23	*	60	—	2	—	1	—	2.4 : 10.0	
pper Tubes & Pipes	7,269	1	9	5	50	*	33	—	*	—	1	*	1.3 : 7.3	
ckel Bars, Rods etc.	1,297	2	44	3	46	—	2	—	3	—	*	—	0.3 : 1.3	
ckel Strip, Powders, etc.	1,506	17	12	4	43	—	16	—	—	—	4	—	0.2 : 1.5	
wrought Aluminium	9,224	8	6	37	12	—	1	5	—	—	3	—	0.2 : 9.0	(5)
uminium Bars, Rods, etc.	3,325	5	6	*	40	*	30	—	—	—	18	—	1.2 : 3.3	
uminium Plates, Sheet, Strip etc.	14,383	8	5	12	30	1	34	*	*	—	7	*	2.0 : 14.4	
ad, Unwrought	7,122	1	1	—	7	—	30	—	—	—	—	—	1.5 : 7.1	(6)
nc, Unwrought	3,471	—	*	4	13	—	26	2	—	—	—	—	4.9 : 3.5	
n, Unwrought	7,530	*	32	—	2	—	8	—	—	—	—	—	11.7 : 7.5	(7)
gnesium, Unwrought and Wrought	344	50	9	—	—	—	—	18	—	—	—	—	0.1 : 0.3	
her Non-ferrous metal products	2,475	11	19	5	9	—	19	—	—	—	—	—	2.9 : 2.5	
IEMICALS AND CHEMICAL PRODUCTS														
neral and Chemical Fertilizers														
trogenous	3,561	—	—	6	82	—	12	—	—	—	—	—	16.0 : 3.5	
osphatic	4,836	40	—	2	4	—	43	—	—	—	—	—	13.4 : 4.8	
tassic	7,959	—	—	9	35	—	26	—	—	—	—	—	Neg. : 8.0	(8)
ints & Varnishes	6,263	6	22	1	40	1	19	3	*	4	2	—	17.4 : 6.2	
nthetic Organic Dyestuffs	14,514	4	12	2	40	*	3	—	—	2	20	—	5.4 : 14.5	
tists Colours	105	4	50	—	38	1	—	—	—	—	—	—	0.8 : 0.1	
ap	2,156	*	14	4	20	*	62	—	—	—	—	—	1.5 : 2.1	
rfumery & Cosmetics	6,818	2	24	24	28	*	39	—	—	*	2	—	4.0 : 6.8	
lishes, Waxes, etc.	1,775	3	15	1	27	*	48	—	*	1	4	—	1.1 : 1.8	
face-acting Washing preps.	9,134	7	11	1	19	*	57	*	*	—	3	—	4.9 : 9.1	
armaceutical Products														
dicaments	14,415	4	12	11	12	2	30	*	1	5	21	*	24.0 : 14.0	
dding, Gauze, etc.	707	1	7	2	49	—	35	1	—	3	—	—	12.0 : 0.7	
sinfectants, Insecticides, etc.	3,308	3	15	2	45	6	19	—	*	3	4	—	20.0 : 3.3	

Where a dash is shown imports are nil or negligible.   * Where an asterisk is shown imports are less than 1 per cent.

tes: Other exporting countries include:

(1) U.S.S.R. 82%.   (3) Czechoslovakia 3%.   (5) U.S.S.R. 11%, Canada 10%.   (7) China 45%.
(2) East Germany 2%.   (4) East Germany 8%.   (6) Mexico 24%.   (8) North Africa 15%.

Product Group and Product	Total Imports $'000	\multicolumn{11}{c}{Suppliers' Percentage Share of Imports}	Export/ Import Ratio ($ million)	Notes
		U.S.	U.K.	Fr.	Ger.	It.	Bel/ Lux.	Nor.	Swe.	Den.	Switz.	Aust.		
		%	%	%	%	%	%	%	%	%	%	%		
PAPER														
Kraft Paper	21,635	4	—	*	2	*	1	4	50	—	—	—	1.5 : 22.0	(1)
Building Board	11,401	*	*	9	10	—	16	3	39	*	*	1	2.2 : 11.4	(2)
Newsprint	13,033	*	—	2	*	—	31	2	19	—	—	—	6.7 : 13.0	(3)
FACTORY PLANT & EQUIPMENT														
Industrial Machinery														
Steam Boilers	4,506	4	16	—	70	1	6	—	2	2	—	—	1.7 : 4.5	
Aux. Steam Plant	1,270	2	53	*	36	1	5	—	*	*	1	—	0.2 : 1.3	
Refrigerating Equipment	7,896	19	7	4	33	5	11	*	14	3	2	*	2.8 : 8.0	
Air Conditioning Equipment	1,114	39	3	5	22	3	16	—	4	*	7	—	1.1 : 1.1	
Heating Plant	19,907	7	8	5	55	4	8	*	3	3	3	1	19.0 : 20.0	
Pumping M/c for Liquids	16,571	12	17	3	42	1	11	1	5	2	4	1	9.5 : 16.6	
Pumping M/c for Air and Vacuum	15,297	6	18	3	37	2	8	*	6	2	15	2	2.6 : 15.0	
Centrifugal M/c.	14,944	5	10	2	64	1	9	*	4	1	2	*	5.4 : 15.0	
Production Machinery														
Pulp & Paper Machinery	10,007	6	7	2	54	9	12	*	1	—	5	*	3.5 : 10.0	
Textile Weaving and Knitting Machinery	8,559	8	6	2	42	*	14	—	5	*	20	*	0.9 : 8.5	
Machine Tools for Metal Working	25,844	5	8	7	45	8	6	*	*	*	1	*	10.8 : 26.0	
Rolling Mills Equipment	7,566	38	19	*	32	—	10	—	*	*	—	*	1.2 : 7.5	
Welding Plant	604	4	5	3	74	—	*	—	7	—	4	*	0.1 : 0.6	
Spinning and Doubling M/c.	7,857	16	10	7	49	2	6	—	—	—	10	—	0.6 : 7.9	
Packaging Machinery & Bottling Plant	11,217	11	16	3	59	2	15	*	2	*	—	—	5.0 : 11.2	
Pneumatic M/c. Tools	2,119	28	16	1	22	—	9	—	14	—	2	1	0.7 : 2.1	
Engineering Supplies														
Sandpaper, Emery paper, etc.	2,001	18	13	1	49	*	*	1	1	*	12	—	0.2 : 2.0	
Refractory Goods	637	4	19	10	62	1	3	—	—	—	*	*	0.1 : 0.6	
Fabricated Asbestos	2,173	5	61	2	19	*	11	—	*	*	*	*	0.5 : 2.1	
Ball Bearings	9,088	11	9	3	27	7	2	—	35	1	2	2	3.8 : 9.0	
Rubber Belting	2,146	16	18	4	26	18	15	3	2	8	*	*	1.5 : 2.1	
Textile Belting	651	1	68	*	24	—	2	—	*	—	4	—	0.2 : 0.7	
Transmission Shafts, Gears, etc.	26,392	8	14	4	50	1	10	*	3	1	5	1	7.0 : 26.0	
Taps, Cocks, Valves, etc.	23,187	15	20	4	42	2	8	*	2	2	4	1	6.2 : 23.0	
Metal Bottle Stoppers	795	4	11	4	25	25	23	—	—	*	—	6	3.7 : 0.8	
ELECTRICAL PLANT														
Generators, Motors etc.	48,136	7	9	7	21	8	23	*	1	3	4	2	23.0 : 48.0	
Electrical Circuit Apparatus	44,740	12	9	8	41	2	13	*	1	1	7	4	24.0 : 45.0	
ELECTRICAL EQUIPMENT														
Insulating Cable and Wire	12,297	8	6	3	43	*	36	—	*	*	1	—	15.0 : 12.3	
Insulating Fittings	3,638	6	5	6	32	3	38	—	—	—	2	1	1.4 : 3.6	
Electrical Carbons	1,588	6	25	10	29	1	3	—	1	—	15	—	0.4 : 1.6	
Electric/Electronic Measuring Apparatus	61,561	13	5	7	53	*	5	*	*	*	4	*	12.9 : 61.0	
Electro-Magnets	1,606	13	9	6	48	2	4	—	4	—	9	1	2.0 : 1.6	
Electric Filament Lamps	20,510	1	4	8	27	—	48	—	—	—	*	2	45.0 : 20.0	
Accumulators	4,184	4	12	3	32	*	27	—	17	—	2	*	1.6 : 4.2	
Batteries	1,467	1	29	9	33	—	10	—	—	5	*	—	0.5 : 1.5	(4)
Thermionic Cathode Ray Tubes, Transistors, etc.	44,692	na	na	na	na	na	na	na	na	na	na	na	78.0 : 45.0	(5)
Electricity Supply Meters	926	—	—	*	70	—	—	—	—	—	28	—	Neg. : 1.0	

— Where a dash is shown imports are nil or negligible.   * Where an asterisk is shown imports are less than 1 per cent.

Notes: Other exporting countries include:

(1) Finland 37%.   (2) Finland 17%.   (3) Finland 33%.   (4) Japan 7%.   (5) Information classified as secret,

Product Group and Product	Total Imports $'000	Suppliers' Percentage Share of Imports											Export/ Import Ratio ($ million)	Notes
		U.S.	U.K.	Fr.	Ger.	It.	Bel/ Lux.	Nor.	Swe.	Den.	Switz.	Aus.		
		%	%	%	%	%	%	%	%	%	%	%		
TRANSPORT EQUIPMENT														
Motor Cars	177,707	1	4	5	30	6	51	—	1	—	—	—	19.5 : 178.0	
Automobile Parts and Accessories	73,551	10	32	3	33	1	5	—	8	*	*	—	10.0 : 74.0	
Tractors	16,712	*	42	8	39	4	—	—	3	—	*	—	2.3 : 16.7	
EARTH-MOVING MACHINERY														
Excavating, Levelling, etc. Machinery	20,913	30	25	3	26	3	8	*	2	*	*	*	5.0 : 21.0	
Lifting, Handling Machinery etc.	28,513	6	13	6	53	2	9	1	3	1	3	*	12.5 : 28.5	
AUTOMATIC VENDING EQUIPMENT AND WEIGHING MACHINES														
Automatic Vending Machines	1,636	10	4	—	66	—	12	—	2	3	*	—	0.4 : 1.6	
Weighing Machines	2,882	5	6	1	50	*	25	—	*	*	10	*	2.6 : 2.9	
PHOTOGRAPHIC AND OPTICAL GOODS, SCIENTIFIC INSTRUMENTS AND SUPPLIES														
Cameras	4,952	5	4	*	59	1	3	—	*	—	4	—	0.6 : 5.0	(1)
Lenses, Unmounted and Mounted	2,420	40	7	6	26	—	2	—	—	—	7	*	0.8 : 2.4	
Microscopes	928	5	2	*	51	*	—	—	—	—	6	5	Neg.: 1.0	
Surveying Instruments	2,774	20	20	1	32	*	*	1	2	3	10	*	1.0 : 2.8	
Electro-Medical and X-Ray Apparatus	5,079	8	5	3	40	10	23	—	1	2	3	*	18.6 : 5.0	
Manometers, Thermostats etc.	6,139	20	25	4	30	2	4	—	1	8	4	*	10.3 : 6.1	
Drawing Instruments	3,883	8	9	4	49	2	5	—	3	2	7	*	1.4 : 3.9	
Photographic Chemicals	766	22	10	1	30	*	36	—	—	—	—	—	0.6 : 0.8	
Photographic Films	4,940	25	9	2	32	3	27	—	—	—	*	—	0.2 : 5.0	
Photographic Paper	3,036	7	6	1	38	*	47	—	—	—	—	—	4.8 : 3.0	
PLASTICS														
Products of Condensation	19,597	19	16	5	40	1	11	—	3	1	2	*	19.0 : 19.0	
Products of Polymerisation	36,685	7	11	6	35	9	22	*	1	1	1	*	19.0 : 37.0	
Plastic Manufactures	19,527	4	5	5	36	5	35	*	1	3	3	*	11.0 : 20.0	
OFFICE EQUIPMENT														
Typewriters	4,814	7	3	1	65	12	—	—	2	—	5	—	20.0 : 5.0	
Electronic Calculating Machines	3,652	66	10	—	22	1	—	—	—	*	—	—	1.2 : 3.6	
Other Accounting Machines	7,797	10	12	1	36	17	—	*	13	—	6	*	10.6 : 7.8	
Punched Card Machines	11,816	12	8	38	32	3	1	—	2	—	—	—	4.2 : 11.8	
Duplicating Machines	483	2	48	—	35	2	—	—	*	11	*	—	1.1 : 0.5	
TOOLS AND IMPLEMENTS														
Band Saws	3,856	50	8	*	25	*	5	1	7	*	1	—	1.1 : 3.9	
Hand Tools, Pliers, Spanners, Snips, etc.	4,933	14	5	2	58	2	*	*	9	—	2	1	2.7 : 5.0	
Electric Hand Tools	3,707	26	13	3	40	*	13	—	*	*	3	—	2.4 : 3.7	
Other Hand Tools	5,333	9	10	3	55	2	3	—	5	1	2	*	0.9 : 5.3	

Where a dash is shown imports are nil or negligible.   * Where an asterisk is shown imports are less than 1 per cent.

Notes: Other exporting countries include:

(1) Japan 17%.

Product Group and Product	Total Imports ($'000)	Suppliers' Percentage Share of Imports											Export/ Import Ratio ($ million)	Notes
		U.S.	U.K.	Fr.	Ger.	It.	Bel/ Lux.	Nor.	Swe.	Den.	Switz.	Aus.		
		%	%	%	%	%	%	%	%	%	%	%		
TEXTILES AND CLOTHING														
Woven & Knitted Fabrics														
Woollen Fabrics	39,704	*	9	5	10	25	48	–	–	–	–	–	30.0 : 40.0	
Cotton Fabrics, bleached and unbleached	43,587	*	2	12	16	2	40	–	*	*	2	1	81.0 : 44.0	(1)
Linen Fabrics	579	*	18	3	11	1	56	–	2	5	3	–	0.3 : 0.6	
Fabrics of Man-made Fibres, (Synthetic and Artificial)	47,799	2	2	3	27	12	38	–	*	*	2	*	32.0 : 48.0	
Knitted Fabrics	16,020	4	3	2	42	1	40	–	2	–	*	*	27.6 : 16.0	
Narrow Fabrics	2,104	3	4	4	31	4	45	–	1	*	3	–	1.0 : 2.1	
Clothing														
Leather Footwear	19,946	*	3	3	14	34	32	*	*	–	3	–	11.5 : 20.0	
Knitted Outerwear	46,145	*	2	3	6	29	44	*	*	–	1	*	7.7 : 46.0	
Knitted Underwear	7,358	3	2	2	19	6	56	*	*	*	1	–	4.0 : 7.4	
Mens Underwear	4,792	2	1	*	3	1	75	–	1	–	1	–	1.8 : 4.8	
Mens Outerwear	17,966	1	2	1	45	5	35	*	1	*	*	–	14.0 : 18.0	
Womens Outerwear	31,412	2	6	3	30	6	39	–	1	–	4	*	25.0 : 31.0	
Womens Underwear	1,057	8	4	5	21	1	43	–	–	–	1	–	0.9 : 1.0	
Stockings	11,220	*	*	2	20	20	52	2	–	–	*	*	4.5 : 11.2	
Corsetry	5,077	9	7	3	24	*	44	2	2	1	*	6	3.2 : 5.0	
HOUSEHOLD AND CONSUMER DURABLES														
Domestic Refrigerators	17,857	*	*	17	47	30	2	–	*	–	*	–	Neg.: 17.9	
Domestic Washing Machines	14,558	1	5	9	72	8	4	–	–	–	–	–	3.1 : 14.6	
Electric Domestic Appliances	5,185	1	12	11	49	*	9	*	5	2	7	–	11.7 : 5.2	
Carpets	13,863	*	2	*	1	*	94	–	–	*	*	*	11.7 : 13.9	
Linoleum	2,047	–	5	48	10	–	34	–	–	–	2	–	8.4 : 2.0	
Sewing Machines	10,431	11	7	*	40	5	6	–	5	*	6	*	2.8 : 10.4	
Household Glassware	6,037	2	2	23	19	9	32	*	2	*	*	*	1.1 : 6.0	
Household Chinaware	5,904	–	4	*	67	*	5	–	*	*	*	–	0.2 : 5.9	(2)
Bed and Table Linen	7,221	*	1	1	19	*	72	–	*	*	*	–	5.7 : 7.2	
Electric Razors	3,555	13	22	38	14	*	1	–	–	3	*	1	19.0 : 3.5	
Spoons and Forks	1,147	–	*	1	16	2	6	*	2	*	1	5	1.5 : 1.2	(3)
Knives	1,693	*	1	4	53	5	5	–	2	–	2	1	0.6 : 1.7	
Scissors	601	–	1	*	76	19	–	–	–	–	–	–	Neg.: 0.6	
Aluminium Domestic Utensils	1,763	*	8	6	35	9	14	*	13	–	6	1	0.5 : 1.8	
Brushware	2,604	3	10	6	39	3	20	3	2	*	4	1	1.2 : 2.6	
WATCHES AND CLOCKS														
Watches	2,366	*	*	6	34	1	–	–	–	–	56	–	Neg.: 2.4	
Clocks	2,346	*	8	1	76	1	1	–	*	–	4	–	0.5 : 2.4	
MISCELLANEOUS METAL MANUFACTURES													Neg.: 2.4 0.5 : 2.4	
Locks, etc.	2,259	*	3	4	69	13	5	–	2	*	*	–	0.4 : 2.3	
Safes, etc.	134	–	7	–	72	–	15	–	–	–	–	–	0.2 : 0.1	
Iron and Steel Chain	6,782	8	17	2	54	4	6	–	3	*	*	*	1.4 : 6.8	
Iron and Steel Springs	3,338	7	6	6	31	*	18	–	7	–	8	14	0.5 : 3.4	
RUBBER MANUFACTURES														
Tyres	14,913	4	5	5	24	7	50	–	2	–	*	2	24.0 : 15.0	
General Rubber Manufactures	4,849	22	19	6	33	2	9	–	3	2	2	–	2.0 : 4.9	

– Where a dash is shown imports are nil or negligible.   * Where an asterisk is shown imports are less than 1 per cent.

Notes: Other exporting countries include:

(1) China 25%.   (2) Japan 14%.   (3) Japan 68%.

Product Group and Product	Total Imports $'000	Suppliers' Percentage Share of Imports											Export/Import Ratio ($ million)	Notes
		U.S.	U.K.	Fr.	Ger.	It.	Bel/Lux.	Nor.	Swe.	Den.	Switz	Aus.		
		%	%	%	%	%	%	%	%	%	%	%		
…DIO AND TELEVISION														
…nophones, Tape Machines, …tc.	41,643	*	*	*	*	*	1	*	—	—	*	—	33.0 : 42.0	(1)
…nophone Records	6,156	5	8	5	22	3	3	—	—	—	1	*	5.7 : 6.1	(2)
…io Receivers	78,157	*	2	5	20	3	55	—	1	1	2	2	54.0 : 78.0	(3)
…evision Receivers														
…CELLANEOUS …ANUFACTURES														
…uum Flasks	489	2	4	*	39	—	32	—	1	—	*	*	Neg.: 0.5	
… Manufactures	146	—	—	—	—	4	93	—	—	—	—	—	0.4 : 0.1	
…f Aids	227	—	*	—	72	—	—	—	5	11	*	5	1.0 : 0.2	
…nt Sprays	231	*	*	36	48	*	—	—	—	—	—	8	1.0 : 0.2	
…bs	687	*	2	2	59	*	11	—	8	—	1	11	Neg.: 0.7	
…ss Buttons	1,306	2	2	3	45	34	*	—	*	1	*	*	2.0 : 1.3	
…kers Pipes	431	1	9	29	9	21	8	—	—	1	—	1	0.2 : 0.4	
…hters	1,683	1	11	18	13	*	4	—	*	—	5	8	1.0 : 1.7	
…hion Jewellery	1,364	2	2	2	38	7	1	—	—	*	*	12	1.0 : 1.4	
…cils	642	2	6	*	47	*	*	—	2	*	17	7	0.2 : 0.6	
…ntain Pens	2,876	10	6	2	44	10	15	—	5	*	1	—	0.2 : 2.9	
…ls	1,201	*	3	5	16	48	16	—	—	—	*	—	0.2 : 1.2	
…s	10,300	3	12	7	39	6	4	*	*	4	*	*	3.0 : 10.3	
…OD MANUFACTURES														
…cuits and Cakes	6,933	*	3	1	2	*	92	—	—	*	—	*	18.4 : 6.9	
…s, Jellies etc.	453	*	7	*	—	—	88	—	—	—	—	—	1.0 : 0.4	
…ar Confectionery	2,758	*	20	1	4	5	51	—	*	*	*	*	13.9 : 2.7	
…colate Preparations	6,270	—	*	1	2	*	64	—	*	—	*	—	17.9 : 6.3	
…served Fruits, other than …ried	8,590	50	*	*	*	*	8	—	—	—	—	—	6.3 : 8.6	(4)
…ps	998	*	7	2	31	*	52	—	—	—	6	—	7.1 : 1.0	
…ces	641	11	11	2	22	5	15	—	—	—	14	—	1.2 : 0.6	
…ese	2,060	—	8	20	3	3	29	2	—	3	12	*	70.0 : 2.0	
…densed Milk	—	—	—	—	—	—	—	—	—	—	—	—	94.0 : Neg.	
…ed Fruits	6,861	14	—	3	—	—	—	—	—	—	—	—	0.2 : 6.9	(5)
…nflakes, Puffed Rice, …tc.	75	10	65	—	—	—	—	—	—	20	—	—	0.5 : 0.1	
…OKS AND PRINTED …ATTER														
…ks, Brochures and …amphlets	6,520	13	16	20	16	2	24	—	—	—	2	—	12.6 : 6.5	
…wspapers, Journals and …eriodicals	4,058	12	14	17	25	*	26	—	—	—	1	*	5.4 : 4.0	
…TAL IMPORTS …L PRODUCTS and …ERCENTAGE SHARES	$ million 5,967	11	7	5	24	3	19	*	3	*	2	*		

Where a dash is shown imports are nil or negligible.   * Where an asterisk is shown imports are less than 1 per cent.

…tes: Other exporting countries include:

(1) Japan 2%, Secret 95%.   (3) Included in Radio.   (5) Spain 1%, Greece 33%, Turkey 33%,
(2) Secret 50%.   (4) China, Japan, Hong Kong, etc. 40%.   Iran 12%, Australia 2%.

Product Group and Product	Total Imports $'000	Suppliers' Percentage Share of Imports											Export/ Import Ratio ($ million)	Notes
		U.S.	U.K.	Fr.	Ger.	It.	Neth.	Nor.	Swe.	Den.	Switz.	Aust.		
		%	%	%	%	%	%	%	%	%	%	%		
E METALS														
and Steel														
...ms & Billets	9,136	–	*	5	58	*	5	*	3	–	–	–	29.4 : 9.0	(1)
...& Steel coils for -rolling	21,838	–	3	*	3	–	56	–	–	–	–	10	27.0 : 22.0	(2)
...& Steel wire rod	17,064	–	–	33	29	–	17	–	8	–	–	–	34.0 : 17.0	(3)
...l Bars	7,002	–	2	37	48	–	10	–	–	–	–	–	160.0 : 7.0	
...l Angles, Shapes and ...ctions	6,841	–	7	41	38	–	7	–	–	–	–	–	153.0 : 7.0	
...& Steel Sheet, heavy	10,050	–	4	18	53	–	9	–	3	*	–	3	32.0 : 10.0	
...& Steel Sheet, medium	3,183	–	–	20	50	1	28	–	–	–	–	1	17.0 : 3.0	
...& Steel Sheet, thin	8,830	–	3	44	23	1	14	*	*	–	–	3	130.0 : 8.8	
...Plate	1,248	7	58	1	9	–	24	–	–	–	–	–	30.0 : 1.3	
...& Steel Wire	1,328	4	24	5	55	*	8	–	1	–	3	–	43.0 : 1.3	
...less Tubes and Pipes	6,619	–	8	17	42	–	15	–	13	–	–	–	7.3 : 6.6	
...ed Tubes and Pipes	2,830	1	3	5	54	*	24	–	4	*	7	–	24.0 : 2.8	
... & Pipe Fittings	5,388	5	8	16	49	1	5	–	4	*	10	*	2.3 : 5.4	
Ferrous Metals														
...er Bars, Rods, etc.	2,661	2	2	5	46	–	35	–	–	–	4	*	22.5 : 2.6	
...er Plates, Sheets, Strip, ...c.	1,402	12	4	8	26	2	27	–	20	–	1	–	16.3 : 1.4	
...er Tubes & Pipes	2,348	1	11	33	32	*	17	–	–	–	1	1	6.0 : 2.3	
...el Bars, Rods etc.	1,315	59	20	9	7	–	1	–	–	–	2	–	Neg.: 1.3	
...el Strip, Powders, etc.	473	32	30	14	14	–	5	–	–	–	3	–	0.3 : 0.5	
...rought Aluminium	42,050	5	*	76	1	–	2	2	–	–	*	–	0.4 : 42.0	(4)
...inium Bars, Rods, etc.	1,656	11	21	6	35	–	14	–	–	–	11	–	8.0 : 1.6	
...inium Plates, Sheet, Strip ...c.	11,869	4	8	22	33	*	23	*	*	–	6	*	16.3 : 11.9	
...d, Unwrought	3,176	13	6	–	17	–	33	–	–	–	–	–	12.5 : 3.1	
...s, Unwrought	5,301	–	*	*	11	–	3	*	–	–	–	–	27.0 : 5.3	(5)
... Unwrought	6,437	–	9	–	3	–	41	–	–	–	–	–	16.0 : 6.5	(6)
...nesium, Unwrought and ...ought	396	17	5	–	–	5	–	20	–	–	–	–	– –	
...r Non-ferrous metal ...oducts	24,126	1	1	1	*	–	2	–	–	–	–	–	25.0 : 24.0	(7)
MICALS AND CHEMICAL RODUCTS														
eral and Chemical ertilizers														
...ogenous	4,520	–	–	42	49	–	2	–	–	–	*	–	26.0 : 4.5	
...sphatic	Neg.												32.0 : Neg.	
...assic	40,360	–	–	80	8	–	–	–	–	–	–	–	42.0 : 40.0	(8)
...ts & Varnishes	8,060	10	11	5	33	*	39	*	*	*	*	–	4.9 : 8.0	
...hetic Organic Dyestuffs	13,495	6	11	7	45	2	6	–	–	*	19	–	2.8 : 13.5	
...sts Colours	437	2	8	2	36	–	46	–	–	–	–	–	Neg.: 0.4	
...	1,021	1	6	13	26	1	52	–	–	–	1	–	1.1 : 1.0	
...umery & Cosmetics	5,629	2	15	34	18	3	26	–	–	–	2	–	2.2 : 5.6	
...shes, Waxes, etc.	1,842	6	14	11	37	*	25	–	*	*	5	–	1.1 : 1.8	
...ace-acting Washing preps.	4,405	17	5	10	39	–	22	*	*	–	5	–	12.7 : 4.4	
rmaceutical Products														
...icaments	28,104	13	6	10	15	2	26	*	*	2	24	*	18.0 : 28.0	
...ding, Gauze, etc.	871	6	25	21	36	*	7	–	–	2	–	–	0.5 : 0.9	
...nfectants, Insecticides, ...c.	2,959	3	3	8	43	2	32	–	*	*	7	–	2.5 : 3.0	

...here a dash is shown imports are nil or negligible.   * Where an asterisk is shown imports are less than 1 per cent.

...es: Other exporting countries include:

   (1)   U.S.S.R., Poland, Rumania 28%.   (4)   U.S.S.R. 3%, Canada 4%.   (7)   Congo 92%.
   (2)   Japan 22%.   (5)   Congo 24%, Australia 40%.   (8)   East Germany, U.S.S.R. 7%.
   (3)   Japan 5%.   (6)   Congo 45%.

Product Group and Product	Total Imports $'000	Suppliers' Percentage Share of Imports											Export/Import Ratio ($ million)	Note
		U.S.	U.K.	Fr.	Ger.	It.	Neth.	Nor.	Swe.	Den.	Switz.	Aust.		
		%	%	%	%	%	%	%	%	%	%	%		
PAPER														
Kraft Paper	15,477	4	—	3	1	*	4	3	46	—	—	—	1.2 : 15.5	(1)
Building Board	3,232	10	*	2	19	*	18	*	27	*	*	1	2.8 : 3.2	(2)
Newsprint	10,218	—	—	5	*	—	49	8	8	—	—	—	6.4 : 10.0	(3)
FACTORY PLANT & EQUIPMENT														
Industrial Machinery														
Steam Boilers	1,981	26	6	10	28	5	20	—	*	—	2	2	2.1 : 2.0	
Aux. Steam Plant	673	4	5	23	52	2	8	—	—	—	4	—	0.3 : 0.7	
Refrigerating Equipment	5,418	23	6	8	30	4	8	2	16	3	*	—	2.0 : 5.4	
Air Conditioning Equipment	1,683	28	12	4	28	3	8	*	4	3	10	—	0.3 : 1.7	
Heating Plant	11,857	7	6	19	48	4	9	—	2	3	2	—	6.0 : 12.0	
Pumping M/c for Liquids	11,003	19	10	13	36	1	9	*	5	2	4	1	4.6 : 11.0	
Pumping M/c for Air and Vacuum	13,400	14	7	13	30	2	5	—	6	3	14	2	6.7 : 13.4	
Centrifugal M/c.	6,814	2	10	14	39	3	8	*	8	*	4	*	2.0 : 7.0	
Production Machinery														
Pulp & Paper Machinery	5,147	27	11	11	32	4	10	*	1	—	1	*	1.5 : 5.1	
Textile Weaving and Knitting Machinery	10,521	9	12	9	29	8	5	—	1	*	23	*	16.9 : 10.0	
Machine Tools for Metal Working	24,052	6	8	12	48	6	6	*	1	*	4	*	20.0 : 24.0	
Rolling Mills Equipment	13,408	5	19	12	49	5	1	—	7	—	*	*	9.5 : 13.4	
Welding Plant	500	3	5	40	38	—	—	—	2	—	8	*	Neg.: 0.5	
Spinning and Doubling M/c.	13,766	7	18	18	28	8	1	—	—	—	18	—	12.5 : 13.7	
Packaging Machinery & Bottling Plant	6,230	9	7	15	42	3	15	*	1	*	—	—	9.0 : 6.0	
Pneumatic M/c. Tools	4,307	63	5	2	17	—	2	—	7	—	*	*	3.0 : 4.3	
Engineering Supplies														
Sandpaper, Emery paper, etc.	2,120	27	5	13	34	4	5	*	1	*	9	—	Neg.: 2.1	
Refractory Goods	1,007	1	13	18	54	1	4	—	—	—	*	6	0.2 : 1.0	
Fabricated Asbestos	1,223	11	46	8	14	—	8	—	*	*	1	10	0.6 : 1.2	
Ball Bearings	9,898	16	5	5	28	7	5	—	26	—	2	2	0.3 : 10.0	
Rubber Belting	3,191	16	21	13	16	21	14	2	2	10	2	—	1.0 : 3.0	
Textile Belting	447	4	28	41	10	3	11	—	—	—	2	—	0.3 : 0.5	
Transmission Shafts, Gears, etc.	13,025	12	11	10	46	1	10	—	2	1	4	*	6.0 : 13.0	
Taps, Cocks, Valves, etc.	17,537	13	12	12	39	3	11	—	2	1	2	2	5.3 : 17.5	
Metal Bottle Stoppers	1,771	14	13	17	11	21	22	—	—	*	—	*	2.9 : 1.8	
ELECTRICAL PLANT														
Generators, Motors etc.	31,820	9	3	13	30	1	26	—	8	*	5	*	28.0 : 32.0	
Electrical Circuit Apparatus	35,142	18	4	14	32	3	19	*	2	*	5	*	13.7 : 35.0	
ELECTRICAL EQUIPMENT														
Insulating Cable and Wire	11,600	7	3	9	37	2	33	—	5	*	4	—	10.0 : 11.6	
Insulating Fittings	2,494	3	3	23	24	2	30	—	—	—	10	*	2.0 : 2.5	
Electrical Carbons	1,585	7	6	18	33	*	3	—	—	—	1	—	0.1 : 1.6	
Electric/Electronic Measuring Apparatus	18,217	47	8	4	20	1	8	*	1	*	5	*	3.2 : 18.0	
Electro-Magnets	1,962	7	9	11	29	*	40	—	*	—	2	1	0.2 : 2.0	
Electric Filament Lamps	6,861	5	4	2	16	—	67	—	—	—	*	*	6.5 : 6.8	
Accumulators	2,997	9	8	11	34	2	30	—	3	—	2	—	2.3 : 3.0	
Batteries	1,960	1	11	20	36	*	11	—	—	14	—	—	Neg.: 2.0	(4)
Thermionic Cathode Ray Tubes, Transistors, etc.	18,421	14	3	4	9	1	67	—	—	—	*	*	7.0 : 18.0	
Electricity Supply Meters	1,417	*	—	2	43	—	—	—	—	—	53	—	0.1 : 1.4	

— Where a dash is shown imports are nil or negligible.   * Where an asterisk is shown imports are less than 1 per cent.

Notes: Other exporting countries include:

(1) Finland 37%. (2) Finland 15%. (3) Finland 18%. (4) Japan 5%.

Product Group and Product	Total Imports ($'000)	Suppliers' Percentage Share of Imports											Export/ Import Ratio ($ million)	Notes
		U.S.	U.K.	Fr.	Ger.	It.	Neth.	Nor.	Swe.	Den.	Switz.	Aus.		
		%	%	%	%	%	%	%	%	%	%	%		
TILES AND CLOTHING														
en & Knitted Fabrics														
len Fabrics	23,703	*	15	16	19	15	34	—	*	*	*	*	32.0 : 24.0	
on Fabrics, bleached and bleached	26,086	6	2	15	14	4	49	—	—	—	1	*	52.0 : 26.0	
n Fabrics	279	*	39	18	15	2	12	—	*	*	7	—	11.5 : 0.3	
ics of Man-made Fibres, ynthetic and Artificial)	39,591	4	*	20	28	10	27	—	—	—	12	*	46.0 : 40.0	
ted Fabrics	10,456	1	*	10	13	3	72	—	—	—	*	*	12.3 : 10.4	
ow Fabrics	1,841	5	10	21	18	7	19	—	—	—	17	—	1.6 : 1.8	
hing														
her Footwear	21,117	*	2	18	12	39	16	*	*	—	4	—	12.6 : 21.0	
ted Outerwear	11,283	*	5	31	5	27	21	*	*	—	2	2	32.0 : 11.0	
ted Underwear	4,133	1	2	25	10	7	40	—	—	—	8	2	2.6 : 4.0	
s Underwear	2,152	2	3	7	2	*	58	—	—	—	4	9	6.4 : 2.1	
s Outerwear	9,835	*	3	10	17	7	56	*	*	*	2	2	16.0 : 9.8	
ens Outerwear	13,984	*	2	19	8	5	45	—	—	—	1	*	20.0 : 14.0	
ens Underwear	964	4	1	17	7	3	35	—	—	—	5	20	1.5 : 1.0	
kings	9,532	*	*	17	18	22	36	*	—	—	*	*	6.5 : 9.5	
etry	3,080	14	2	16	21	*	36	—	*	*	*	6	2.9 : 3.0	
SEHOLD AND CONSUMER URABLES														
estic Refrigerators	11,651	2	3	74	24	33	*	—	*	—	*	—	1.0 : 11.6	
estic Washing Machines	6,944	4	18	17	49	9	2	—	—	—	*	—	1.3 : 7.0	
tric Domestic Appliances	5,546	2	24	20	19	5	17	*	5	2	4	—	1.6 : 5.5	
ets	3,605	*	7	15	13	*	54	—	—	*	*	*	68.5 : 3.6	
leum	3,662	—	6	34	12	—	47	—	—	—	1	—	3.2 : 3.6	
ing Machines	7,632	11	7	1	34	4	9	—	1	*	15	—	1.6 : 7.6	
sehold Glassware	4,719	2	3	33	26	15	3	*	*	*	*	1	8.3 : 4.7	
sehold Chinaware	3,322	—	*	9	60	*	5	—	*	*	*	—	0.6 : 3.3	(1)
and Table Linen	1,525	1	1	14	21	2	54	—	*	*	2	—	12.8 : 1.5	
tric Razors	1,256	3	5	14	15	6	56	—	—	—	2	*	0.1 : 1.3	
ns and Forks	1,768	—	7	17	33	5	24	*	*	1	1	2	0.2 : 1.8	
ves	1,382	*	4	18	47	7	14	—	*	*	1	2	0.1 : 1.4	
sors	459	—	*	10	60	23	5	—	—	—	—	—	Neg.: 0.5	
ninium Domestic Utensils	1,541	*	15	13	28	6	24	*	*	—	5	*	0.4 : 1.5	
shware	2,132	3	8	18	30	2	32	*	*	*	2	*	1.1 : 2.1	
TCHES AND CLOCKS														
hes	4,866	*	*	6	20	—	—	—	—	—	73	—	0.1 : 5.0	
cks	2,088	*	5	10	69	*	4	—	*	—	6	—	Neg.: 2.0	
CELLANEOUS METAL ANUFACTURES														
ks, etc.	1,854	5	3	10	58	10	10	—	*	—	2	—	0.4 : 1.9	
s, etc.	204	*	7	29	44	—	17	—	—	—	—	—	Neg.: 0.2	
and Steel Chain	3,377	6	25	8	50	2	4	—	*	*	*	—	1.0 : 3.4	
and Steel Springs	1,484	15	10	11	4	2	21	—	1	—	3	—	1.3 : 1.5	
BER MANUFACTURES														
es	21,230	6	7	15	14	8	47	—	*	—	1	*	20.0 : 21.0	
eral Rubber Manufactures	4,721	13	17	17	29	3	13	—	1	*	2	*	1.0 : 4.7	

here a dash is shown imports are nil or negligible.   * Where an asterisk is shown imports are less than 1 per cent.

es: Other exporting countries include:

(1) Japan 13%.

Product Group and Product	Total Imports $'000	Suppliers' Percentage Share of Imports											Export/ Import Ratio ($ million)	Note
		U.S.	U.K.	Fr.	Ger.	It.	Neth.	Nor.	Swe.	Den.	Switz.	Aus.		
		%	%	%	%	%	%	%	%	%	%	%		
TRANSPORT EQUIPMENT														
Motor Cars	60,797	3	8	21	46	8	10	–	*	–	–	–	146.0 : 61.0	
Automobile Parts and Accessories	285,405	6	12	25	34	4	1	–	3	*	*	1	11.0 : 285.0	
Tractors	15,023	3	26	1	36	1	*	–	1	–	1	2	0.5 : 15.0	
EARTH-MOVING MACHINERY														
Excavating, Levelling, etc. Machinery	24,327	33	22	12	24	*	4	*	2	*	*	*	6.0 : 24.0	
Lifting, Handling Machinery etc.	29,084	16	7	14	47	2	6	*	1	*	3	1	14.0 : 29.0	
AUTOMATIC VENDING EQUIPMENT AND WEIGHING MACHINES														
Automatic Vending Machines	955	34	3	2	47	*	11	–	–	2	*	–	0.5 : 1.0	
Weighing Machines	2,872	7	1	9	55	*	24	–	*	*	2	1	1.9 : 2.9	
PHOTOGRAPHIC AND OPTICAL GOODS, SCIENTIFIC INSTRUMENTS AND SUPPLIES														
Cameras	2,915	5	12	2	58	2	2	–	*	–	2	–	0.2 : 2.9	(1)
Lenses, Unmounted and Mounted	1,414	6	4	23	32	1	7	–	*	–	5	2	0.3 : 1.4	
Microscopes	526	3	4	2	42	–	3	–	–	–	16	8	Neg. : 0.5	
Surveying Instruments	15,892	17	3	*	71	*	3	*	*	*	1	*	1.7 : 16.0	
Electro-Medical and X-Ray Apparatus	2,638	13	2	11	31	5	21	–	3	*	10	*	1.3 : 2.6	
Manometers, Thermostats etc.	5,083	24	12	10	29	1	13	–	1	3	3	2	0.5 : 5.0	
Drawing Instruments	3,699	6	5	15	41	7	8	–	1	1	10	*	0.4 : 3.7	
Photographic Chemicals	386	34	13	4	26	3	18	–	–	–	–	–	2.3 : 0.4	
Photographic Films	1,723	52	4	5	24	6	2	–	–	–	1	–	23.0 : 1.7	
Photographic Paper	2,377	10	3	56	17	–	12	–	–	–	–	–	17.8 : 2.4	
PLASTICS														
Products of Condensation	26,117	6	9	30	30	3	15	–	–	–	1	–	5.4 : 26.0	
Products of Polymerisation	31,117	12	12	12	33	8	2	–	1	*	1	*	13.0 : 31.0	
Plastic Manufactures	13,734	5	4	20	28	4	33	*	*	*	1	*	15.0 : 14.0	
OFFICE EQUIPMENT														
Typewriters	4,116	5	1	14	32	29	9	–	3	–	2	–	0.2 : 4.0	
Electronic Calculating Machines	371	16	17	23	10	*	4	–	16	–	–	–	0.4 : 0.4	
Other Accounting Machines	7,290	7	8	2	27	32	4	*	8	–	4	*	0.5 : 7.3	
Punched Card Machines	12,445	17	8	18	45	2	1	–	2	–	–	–	1.5 : 12.5	
Duplicating Machines	518	3	46	–	32	2	2	–	2	9	*	–	0.2 : 0.5	
TOOLS AND IMPLEMENTS														
Hand Saws	2,113	13	13	5	49	*	3	1	7	1	2	–	1.6 : 2.0	(2)
Hand Tools, Pliers, Spanners, Snips, etc.	3,399	8	4	14	48	3	10	–	4	–	3	2	0.2 : 3.4	
Electric Hand Tools	3,636	8	22	11	43	4	5	–	*	*	4	–	0.6 : 3.6	
Other Hand Tools	3,687	7	9	15	44	3	4	–	5	*	3	2	0.9 : 3.7	

— Where a dash is shown imports are nil or negligible.   * Where an asterisk is shown imports are less than 1 per cent.

Notes: Other exporting countries include:

  (1) Japan 13%.   (2) Canada 14%.

Product Group and Product	Total Imports $'000	Suppliers' Percentage Share of Imports											Export/ Import Ratio ($ million)	Notes
		U.S.	U.K.	Fr.	Ger.	It.	Neth.	Nor.	Swe.	Den.	Switz.	Aus.		
IO AND TELEVISION		%	%	%	%	%	%	%	%	%	%	%		
nophone, Tape Machines, tc.	9,785	35	3	6	18	2	31	*	—	—	2	1	15.4 : 10.0	
nophone Records	5,176	7	10	38	20	1	20	—	—	—	1	*	1.3 : 5.2	
io Receivers	6,720	1	1	11	41	1	30	—	*	*	1	*	18.0 : 6.7	(1)
evision Receivers	1,936	*	*	7	51	—	37	—	—	—	—	—	16.0 : 2.0	
CELLANEOUS ANUFACTURES														
uum Flasks	370	2	35	2	30	*	1	—	1	—	1	*	0.3 : 0.4	
Manufactures	118	7	3	30	20	—	10	—	—	—	—	—	0.3 : 0.1	
f Aids	299	19	6	—	16	—	30	—	—	16	6	6	Neg.: 0.3	
nt Sprays	145	*	*	62	28	2	—	—	—	—	—	*	Neg.: 0.2	
bs	472	2	3	35	38	5	3	—	*	—	9	3	0.1 : 0.5	
ss Buttons	2,162	3	5	21	28	16	13	—	*	1	*	—	Neg.: 2.2	
kers Pipes	282	3	13	31	8	25	4	—	—	*	—	1	0.2 : 0.3	
nters	1,170	*	6	41	10	—	19	—	*	—	*	8	0.2 : 1.2	
hion Jewellery	1,782	1	3	14	32	6	8	—	—	*	*	15	0.3 : 1.8	
cils	741	2	3	14	52	1	10	—	—	—	8	3	Neg.: 0.7	
ntain Pens	3,454	15	4	26	27	19	4	—	*	*	*	—	0.5 : 3.5	
s	1,236	*	1	13	8	54	9	—	—	—	—	*	Neg.: 1.3	
s	7,801	2	11	14	29	6	13	*	*	4	*	*	0.7 : 7.8	
JD MANUFACTURES														
cuits, and Cakes	5,448	*	5	24	3	*	67	*	—	*	*	*	14.0 : 5.5	
s, Jellies, etc.	1,185	*	3	3	*	*	66	—	1	—	5	—	0.7 : 1.2	
ar Confectionery	5,115	5	16	8	8	5	55	—	*	*	*	*	4.1 : 5.1	
colate Preparations	6,336	—	9	8	8	5	64	*	2	—	3	*	11.6 : 6.3	
served Fruits other than ried	9,274	55	*	*	*	3	3	—	—	—	*	—	2.3 : 9.3	(2)
ps	6,649	*	*	2	2	*	94	—	—	—	*	—	0.9 : 6.6	
ces	1,235	2	5	11	20	1	57	—	—	—	3	—	0.1 : 1.2	
ese	24,922	—	*	16	7	3	49	*	—	3	12	1	2.9 : 25.0	
densed Milk	1,114	—	—	—	—	—	98	—	—	*	—	—	1.5 : 1.1	
d Fruits	4,214	33	—	—	—	—	—	—	—	—	—	—	Neg.: 4.2	(3)
nflakes, Puffed Rice, tc.	300	17	17	—	—	—	64	—	—	—	—	—	Neg.: 0.3	
DKS AND PRINTED ATTER														
ks, Brochures and amphlets	13,089	3	1	60	2	1	3	—	—	—	2	—	12.7 : 13.0	
vspapers, Journals and eriodicals	12,599	*	2	50	12	3	31	—	—	—	*	—	1.7 : 12.6	
'AL IMPORTS L PRODUCTS AND ERCENTAGE SHARES	$ million 5,112	9	8	15	19	3	15	*	3	*	2	*		

Where a dash is shown imports are nil or negligible.   * Where an asterisk is shown imports are less than 1 per cent.

tes: Other exporting countries include:

(1) Japan 9%.   (2) Spain 20%, Philippines, Formosa etc. 10%.   (3) Spain 3%, Greece 3%, Turkey 35%, Iran 6%, Australia 4%.

PART II

Trading accounts, extracted from Input/Output statistics, for about eighteen basic industries in the Common Market countries.

PREFACE

The following tables will be useful in a number of ways. They serve as a source of information on the economic structure of these eighteen industries in each Common Market country. They show something of the inter-relationship of production in the different countries. It is possible, for example, to compare each industry's dependence upon sales to other industries with its sales for private and public consumption and export. The main production cost components have been divided into expenditure on raw materials and services, value added in wages and other elements.

Exporters can compare their own trading accounts with those of the industry as a whole in each Common Market country. Firms which are considering establishment in the Common Market can trace the various cost relationships with production values for the same industry in any of the Common Market countries and gain an accurate picture from which to forecast and budget.

Because of the great complexity of the statistical data involved, the study of the Input/Output Ratio is still to some extent experimental. Certain shortcomings have still to be surmounted. It has taken since 1959 to prepare the tables from which the information in this section of the book has been prepared. Systems of statistical calculation vary in different countries. Profits have had to be shown under a miscellaneous heading. All this has led to a considerable degree of approximation justified by the need to simplify an extremely complex subject.

INDEX

	France	West Germany	Italy	Nether-lands	Belgium/ Luxem-bourg
	page	*page*	*page*	*page*	*page*
AGRICULTURAL MACHINERY AND TRACTORS	50	57	68	77	87
CHEMICAL INDUSTRIES INCLUDING FERTILIZERS	47	—	65	74	83
CHEMICALS	48	—	66	74	—
ELECTRICAL MACHINERY	51	58	69	77	88
FOOTWEAR	44	54	62	72	80
GLASS AND GLASS PRODUCTS	48	—	66	75	84
HOSIERY, KNITWEAR AND KNITTED FABRICS	43	53	61	71	79
IRON AND STEEL (BASIC)	49	56	67	75	—
IRON AND STEEL (BLAST FURNACES)	—	—	—	—	85
IRON AND STEEL (NON-E.C.S.C.)	—	56	—	—	—
LEATHER PRODUCTS EXCEPT FOOTWEAR	—	—	63	—	81
MACHINERY OTHER THAN ELECTRIC	51	—	69	—	87
METAL PRODUCTS	50	—	68	76	86
MOTOR VEHICLES	52	58	70	78	88
NON-FERROUS METALS	49	57	67	76	—
PAPER AND PULP	46	54	62	80	—
PLASTICS	45	55	64	73	82
PRINTING AND PUBLISHING	—	—	63	81	—
ROLLING MILLS	—	—	—	—	86
RUBBER AND ASBESTOS	45	55	64	73	82
SCIENTIFIC, PHOTOGRAPHIC, OPTICAL, WATCHES AND CLOCKS	52	59	—	78	88
SOAPS, DETERGENTS AND PERFUMERY	—	—	—	—	84
STEEL MANUFACTURES	—	—	—	—	85
SYNTHETIC MATERIALS AND FIBRES	47	—	65	—	83
SYNTHETIC MATERIALS, FIBRES AND CHEMICALS	—	55	—	—	—
TEXTILES	44	53	—	72	—
WEARING APPAREL	43	53	61	71	79

TABLE 1: FRANCE

Manufacture of Hosiery, Knitwear and Knitted Fabrics

INPUT			OUTPUT		
				$ million	
Purchases of Materials, Services, Transport, etc		58%	Sales to other Industries	39	
			Sales to Persons	304	
			Sales to Government	—	
Value Added			Capital Formation	—	
Wages and Salaries	21%		Stock Variation	—	
Employers' Social Service Payments	6%				
Depreciation	4%		Apparent Consumption		343
Miscellaneous, including Profits	3%		Export		59
Indirect Taxes paid by purchaser	8%	42%			
	$ million				
Value of Production at ex-works price	394	100%			
Imports of similar goods	8				
Total Supply	402		Total Demand		402

Manufacture of Wearing Apparel

INPUT			OUTPUT		
				$ million	
Purchases of Materials, Services, Transport, etc		47%	Sales to other Industries	48	
			Sales to Persons	1,772	
			Sales to Government	2	
Value Added			Capital Formation	—	
Wages and Salaries	18%		Stock Variation	−2	
Employers' Social Service Payments	5%				
Depreciation	1%		Apparent Consumption		1,820
Miscellaneous, including Profits	20%		Export		110
Indirect Taxes paid by purchaser	9%	53%			
	$ million				
Value of Production at ex-works price	1,923	100%			
Imports of similar goods	7				
Total Supply	1,930		Total Demand		1,930

Manufacture of Made-up Textile Goods except Wearing Apparel

INPUT			OUTPUT	
				$ million
Purchases of Materials, Services, Transport, etc		80%	Sales to other Industries	19
			Sales to Persons	176
			Sales to Government	9
Value Added			Capital Formation	—
Wages and Salaries	10%		Stock Variation	—
Employers' Social Service Payments	3%			
Depreciation	1%		Apparent Consumption	204
Miscellaneous, including Profits	2%		Export	25
Indirect Taxes paid by purchaser	4%	20%		
	$ million			
Value of Production at ex-works price	220	100%		
Imports of similar goods	9			
Total Supply	229		Total Demand	229

Manufacture and Repairing of Footwear

INPUT			OUTPUT	
				$ million
Purchases of Materials, Services, Transport, etc		53%	Sales to other Industries	1
			Sales to Persons	420
			Sales to Government	—
Value Added			Capital Formation	—
Wages and Salaries	20%		Stock Variation	14
Employers' Social Service Payments	5%			
Depreciation	2%		Apparent Consumption	435
Miscellaneous, including Profits	14%		Export	44
Indirect Taxes paid by purchaser	6%	47%		
	$ million			
Value of Production at ex-works price	474	100%		
Imports of similar goods	5			
Total Supply	479		Total Demand	479

Manufacture of Rubber and Asbestos Products

INPUT			OUTPUT		
					$ *million*
Purchases of Materials, Services,			Sales to other Industries	523	
Transport, etc		52%	Sales to Persons	39	
			Sales to Government	17	
Value Added			Capital Formation	—	
Wages and Salaries	21%		Stock Variation	6	
Employers' Social Service Payments	5%				
Depreciation	4%		Apparent Consumption		585
Miscellaneous, including Profits	10%		Export		81
Indirect Taxes paid by purchaser	8%	48%			
	$ *million*				
Value of Production at ex-works price	643	100%			
Imports of similar goods	23				
Total Supply	666		Total Demand		666

Manufacture of Plastic Products

INPUT			OUTPUT		
					$ *million*
Purchases of Materials, Services,			Sales to other Industries	297	
Transport, etc		52%	Sales to Persons	36	
			Sales to Government	1	
Value Added			Capital Formation	—	
Wages and Salaries	18%		Stock Variation	—	
Employers' Social Service Payments	4%				
Depreciation	3%		Apparent Consumption		334
Miscellaneous, including Profits	10%		Export		14
Indirect Taxes paid by purchaser	13%	48%			
	$ *million*				
Value of Production at ex-works price	347	100%			
Imports of similar goods	1				
Total Supply	348		Total Demand		348

Manufacture of Pulp

INPUT			OUTPUT		
					$ *million*
Purchases of Materials, Services, Transport, etc		69%	Sales to other Industries	256	
			Sales to Persons	—	
			Sales to Government	—	
Value Added			Capital Formation	—	
Wages and Salaries	8%		Stock Variation	—2	
Employers' Social Service Payments	2%				
Depreciation	4%		Apparent Consumption		254
Miscellaneous, including Profits	8%		Export		5
Indirect Taxes paid by purchaser	9%	31%			
	$ *million*				
Value of Production at ex-works price	166	100%			
Imports of similar goods	93				
Total Supply	259		Total Demand		259

Manufacture of Paper and Paperboard Products

INPUT			OUTPUT		
					$ *million*
Purchases of Materials, Services, Transport, etc		53%	Sales to other Industries	683	
			Sales to Persons	46	
			Sales to Government	32	
Value Added			Capital Formation	—	
Wages and Salaries	20%		Stock Variation	14	
Employers' Social Service Payments	5%				
Depreciation	4%		Apparent Consumption		775
Miscellaneous, including Profits	9%		Export		61
Indirect Taxes paid by purchaser	9%	47%			
	$ *million*				
Value of Production at ex-works price	792	100%			
Imports of similar goods	44				
Total Supply	836		Total Demand		836

Manufacture of Synthetic Materials and Fibres

INPUT			OUTPUT	
				$ *million*
Purchases of Materials, Services, Transport, etc		57%	Sales to other Industries	488
			Sales to Persons	—
			Sales to Government	—
Value Added			Capital Formation	—
Wages and Salaries	14%		Stock Variation	—14
Employers' Social Service Payments	4%			
Depreciation	7%		Apparent Consumption	474
Miscellaneous, including Profits	11%		Export	85
Indirect Taxes paid by purchaser	7%	43%		
	$ *million*			
Value of Production at ex-works price	458	100%		
Imports of similar goods	101			
Total Supply	559		Total Demand	559

Other Basic Chemical Industries, including the Production of Fertilizers

INPUT			OUTPUT	
				$ *million*
Purchases of Materials, Services, Transport, etc		50%	Sales to other Industries	1,131
			Sales to Persons	—
			Sales to Government	13
Value Added			Capital Formation	—
Wages and Salaries	19%		Stock Variation	94
Employers' Social Service Payments	4%			
Depreciation	7%		Apparent Consumption	1,238
Miscellaneous, including Profits	10%		Export	207
Indirect Taxes paid by purchaser	9%	50%		
	$ *million*			
Value of Production at ex-works price	1,229	100%		
Imports of similar goods	216			
Total Supply	1,445		Total Demand	1,445

Manufacture of Chemicals

INPUT			OUTPUT		
					$ million
Purchases of Materials, Services, Transport, etc		53%	Sales to other Industries	467	
			Sales to Persons	807	
			Sales to Government	47	
Value Added			Capital Formation	—	
Wages and Salaries	20%		Stock Variation	24	
Employers' Social Service Payments	5%				
Depreciation	3%		Apparent Consumption		1,345
Miscellaneous, including Profits	8%		Export		209
Indirect Taxes paid by purchaser	11%	47%			
	$ million				
Value of Production at ex-works price	1,487	100%			
Imports of similar goods	67				
Total Supply	1,554		Total Demand		1,554

Manufacture of Glass and Glass Products

INPUT			OUTPUT		
					$ million
Purchases of Materials, Services, Transport, etc		29%	Sales to other Industries	186	
			Sales to Persons	27	
			Sales to Government	1	
Value Added			Capital Formation	—	
Wages and Salaries	30%		Stock Variation	4	
Employers' Social Service Payments	8%				
Depreciation	7%		Apparent Consumption		218
Miscellaneous, including Profits	12%		Export		57
Indirect Taxes paid by purchaser	14%	71%			
	$ million				
Value of Production at ex-works price	263	100%			
Imports of similar goods	12				
Total Supply	275		Total Demand		275

48

Iron and Steel Basic Industries

INPUT			OUTPUT		
					$ million
Purchases of Materials, Services, Transport, etc		65%	Sales to other Industries	1,893	
			Sales to Persons	—	
			Sales to Government	2	
Value Added			Capital Formation	—	
Wages and Salaries	12%		Stock Variation	—117	
Employers' Social Service Payments	4%				
Depreciation	9%		Apparent Consumption		1,778
Miscellaneous, including Profits	5%		Export		571
Indirect Taxes paid by purchaser	5%	35%			
	$ million				
Value of Production at ex-works price	2,062	100%			
Imports of similar goods	287				
Total Supply	2,349		Total Demand		2,349

Production and Manufactures of Non-Ferrous Metals

INPUT			OUTPUT		
					$ million
Purchases of Materials, Services, Transport, etc		56%	Sales to other Industries	835	
			Sales to Persons	—	
			Sales to Government	24	
Value Added			Capital Formation	—	
Wages and Salaries	13%		Stock Variation	—34	
Employers' Social Service Payments	3%				
Depreciation	5%		Apparent Consumption		825
Miscellaneous, including Profits	13%		Export		103
Indirect Taxes paid by purchaser	10%	44%			
	$ million				
Value of Production at ex-works price	673	100%			
Imports of similar goods	255				
Total Supply	928		Total Demand		928

Manufacture of Metallic Products and Furniture, except Machinery

INPUT			OUTPUT		
					$ million
Purchases of Materials, Services, Transport, etc		50%	Sales to other Industries	1,076	
			Sales to Persons	224	
			Sales to Government	48	
Value Added			Capital Formation	69	
Wages and Salaries	23%		Stock Variation	—16	
Employers' Social Service Payments	6%				
Depreciation	4%		Apparent Consumption		1,401
Miscellaneous, including Profits	7%		Export		170
Indirect Taxes paid by purchaser	10%	50%			
	$ million				
Value of Production at ex-works price	1,496	100%			
Imports of similar goods	75				
Total Supply	1,571		Total Demand		1,571

Manufacture of Agricultural Machinery and Tractors

INPUT			OUTPUT		
					$ million
Purchases of Materials, Services, Transport, etc		60%	Sales to other Industries	27	
			Sales to Persons	—	
			Sales to Government	—	
Value Added			Capital Formation	393	
Wages and Salaries	18%		Stock Variation	14	
Employers' Social Service Payments	5%				
Depreciation	3%		Apparent Consumption		434
Miscellaneous, including Profits	8%		Export		29
Indirect Taxes paid by purchaser	6%	40%			
	$ million				
Value of Production at ex-works price	388	100%			
Imports of similar goods	75				
Total Supply	463		Total Demand		463

Manufacture of Other Machinery, except Electrical Machinery

INPUT			OUTPUT		
				$ *million*	
Purchases of Materials, Services,			Sales to other Industries	889	
Transport, etc		46%	Sales to Persons	306	
			Sales to Government	259	
Value Added			Capital Formation	1,988	
Wages and Salaries	26%		Stock Variation	—18	
Employers' Social Service Payments	7%				
Depreciation	5%		Apparent Consumption		3,424
Miscellaneous, including Profits	7%		Export		508
Indirect Taxes paid by purchaser	9%	54%			
	$ *million*				
Value of Production at ex-works price	3,365	100%			
Imports of similar goods	567				
Total Supply	3,932		Total Demand		3,932

Manufacture of Electrical Machinery and Equipment

INPUT			OUTPUT		
				$ *million*	
Purchases of Materials, Services,			Sales to other Industries	535	
Transport, etc		37%	Sales to Persons	226	
			Sales to Government	189	
Value Added			Capital Formation	503	
Wages and Salaries	29%		Stock Variation	46	
Employers' Social Service Payments	7%				
Depreciation	3%		Apparent Consumption		1,499
Miscellaneous, including Profits	12%		Export		195
Indirect Taxes paid by purchaser	12%	63%			
	$ *million*				
Value of Production at ex-works price	1,587	100%			
Imports of similar goods	107				
Total Supply	1,694		Total Demand		1,694

Manufacture and Assembly of Motor Vehicles

INPUT			OUTPUT	
				$ million
Purchases of Materials, Services,			Sales to other Industries	310
Transport, etc		60%	Sales to Persons	466
			Sales to Government	94
Value Added			Capital Formation	567
Wages and Salaries	20%		Stock Variation	46
Employers' Social Service Payments	5%			
Depreciation	6%		Apparent Consumption	1,483
Miscellaneous, including Profits	5%		Export	618
Indirect Taxes paid by purchaser	4%	40%		
	$ million			
Value of Production at ex-works price	2,065	100%		
Imports of similar goods	36			
Total Supply	2,101		Total Demand	2,101

Manufacture of Professional, Scientific, Measuring and Control Instruments; Photographic and Optical Goods; Watches and Clocks

INPUT			OUTPUT	
				$ million
Purchases of Materials, Services,			Sales to other Industries	26
Transport, etc		35%	Sales to Persons	125
			Sales to Government	29
Value Added			Capital Formation	52
Wages and Salaries	29%		Stock Variation	6
Employers' Social Service Payments	7%			
Depreciation	6%		Apparent Consumption	238
Miscellaneous, including Profits	11%		Export	65
Indirect Taxes paid by purchaser	12%	65%		
	$ million			
Value of Production at ex-works price	227	100%		
Imports of similar goods	76			
Total Supply	303		Total Demand	303

TABLE 2: WEST GERMANY

Manufacture and finishing of Textiles, Hosiery, and Knitwear

INPUT			OUTPUT		
					$ million
Purchases of Materials, Services,			Sales to other Industries	2,160	
Transport, etc		55%	Sales to Persons	1,577	
			Sales to Government	—	
Value Added			Capital Formation	56	
Wages and Salaries	25%		Stock Variation	123	
Employers' Social Service Payments	3%				
Depreciation	5%		Apparent Consumption		3,916
Miscellaneous, including Profits	6%		Export		379
Indirect Taxes paid by purchaser	6%	45%			
	$ million				
Value of Production at ex-works price	3,544	100%			
Imports of similar goods	751				
Total Supply	4,295		Total Demand		4,295

Manufacture of Wearing Apparel and made-up Textile Goods

INPUT			OUTPUT		
					$ million
Purchases of Materials, Services,			Sales to other Industries	303	
Transport, etc		61%	Sales to Persons	1,931	
			Sales to Government	—	
Value Added			Capital Formation	—	
Wages and Salaries	19%		Stock Variation	43	
Employers' Social Service Payments	2%				
Depreciation	2%		Apparent Consumption		2,277
Miscellaneous, including Profits	11%		Export		80
Indirect Taxes paid by purchaser	5%	39%			
	$ million				
Value of Production at ex-works price	2,244	100%			
Imports of similar goods	113				
Total Supply	2,357		Total Demand		2,357

Manufacture of Footwear and Leather Goods

INPUT			OUTPUT		
					$ million
Purchases of Materials, Services, Transport, etc		53%	Sales to other Industries	181	
			Sales to Persons	953	
			Sales to Government	—	
Value Added			Capital Formation	16	
Wages and Salaries	22%		Stock Variation	24	
Employers' Social Service Payments	2%				
Depreciation	2%		Apparent Consumption		1,174
Miscellaneous, including Profits	16%		Export		86
Indirect Taxes paid by purchaser	5%	47%			
	$ million				
Value of Production at ex-works price	1,143	100%			
Imports of similar goods	117				
Total Supply	1,260		Total Demand		1,260

Manufacture of Pulp and Paper

INPUT			OUTPUT		
					$ million
Purchases of Materials, Services, Transport, etc		58%	Sales to other Industries	1,624	
			Sales to Persons	97	
			Sales to Government	—	
Value Added			Capital Formation	9	
Wages and Salaries	19%		Stock Variation	48	
Employers' Social Service Payments	2%				
Depreciation	5%		Apparent Consumption		1,778
Miscellaneous, including Profits	10%		Export		96
Indirect Taxes paid by purchaser	6%	42%			
	$ million				
Value of Production at ex-works price	1,498	100%			
Imports of similar goods	376				
Total Supply	1,874		Total Demand		1,874

Manufacture of Rubber and Asbestos Products

INPUT			OUTPUT		
					$ million
Purchases of Materials, Services, Transport, etc		59%	Sales to other Industries	691	
			Sales to Persons	32	
			Sales to Government	—	
Value Added			Capital Formation	7	
Wages and Salaries	20%		Stock Variation	26	
Employers' Social Service Payments	2%				
Depreciation	3%		Apparent Consumption		756
Miscellaneous, including Profits	11%		Export		107
Indirect Taxes paid by purchaser	5%	41%			
		$ million			
Value of Production at ex-works price	804	100%			
Imports of similar goods	59				
Total Supply	863		Total Demand		863

Plastics and Synthetic Materials and Fibres and Chemical Industries

INPUT			OUTPUT		
					$ million
Purchases of Materials, Services, Transport, etc		57%	Sales to other Industries	3,785	
			Sales to Persons	869	
			Sales to Government	—	
Value Added			Capital Formation	109	
Wages and Salaries	18%		Stock Variation	176	
Employers' Social Service Payments	2%				
Depreciation	6%		Apparent Consumption		4,939
Miscellaneous, including Profits	13%		Export		1,430
Indirect Taxes paid by purchaser	4%	43%			
		$ million			
Value of Production at ex-works price	5,668	100%			
Imports of similar goods	701				
Total Supply	6,369		Total Demand		6,369

Iron and Steel Basic Industries

INPUT			OUTPUT		
					$ million
Purchases of Materials, Services,			Sales to other Industries	3,336	
Transport, etc		67%	Sales to Persons	—	
			Sales to Government	—	
Value Added			Capital Formation	46	
Wages and Salaries	15%		Stock Variation	171	
Employers' Social Service Payments	2%				
Depreciation	6%		Apparent Consumption		3,553
Miscellaneous, including Profits	5%		Export		671
Indirect Taxes paid by purchaser	5%	33%			
	$ million				
Value of Production at ex-works price	3,702	100%			
Imports of similar goods	522				
Total Supply	4,224		Total Demand		4,224

Manufacture of Non-ECSC Steel Products and Metallic Products

INPUT			OUTPUT		
					$ million
Purchases of Materials, Services,			Sales to other Industries	3,306	
Transport, etc		57%	Sales to Persons	629	
			Sales to Government	—	
Value Added			Capital Formation	1,460	
Wages and Salaries	21%		Stock Variation	130	
Employers' Social Service Payments	2%				
Depreciation	3%		Apparent Consumption		5,525
Miscellaneous, including Profits	12%		Export		975
Indirect Taxes paid by purchaser	5%	43%			
	$ million				
Value of Production at ex-works price	6,250	100%			
Imports of similar goods	250				
Total Supply	6,500		Total Demand		6,500

Production and Manufacture of Non-Ferrous Metals

INPUT			OUTPUT		
					$ million
Purchases of Materials, Services,			Sales to other Industries	1,614	
Transport, etc		63%	Sales to Persons	—	
			Sales to Government	—	
Value Added			Capital Formation	8	
Wages and Salaries	14%		Stock Variation	73	
Employers' Social Service Payments	2%				
Depreciation	4%		Apparent Consumption		1,695
Miscellaneous, including Profits	13%		Export		254
Indirect Taxes paid by purchaser	4%	37%			
	$ million				
Value of Production at ex-works price	1,179	100%			
Imports of similar goods	770				
Total Supply	1,949		Total Demand		1,949

Manufacture of Agricultural Machinery, Tractors, Non-Electrical Machinery, Railroad Equipment, and Aircraft

INPUT			OUTPUT		
					$ million
Purchases of Materials, Services,			Sales to other Industries	2,679	
Transport, etc		51%	Sales to Persons	430	
			Sales to Government	—	
Value Added			Capital Formation	3,622	
Wages and Salaries	26%		Stock Variation	235	
Employers' Social Service Payments	3%				
Depreciation	3%		Apparent Consumption		6,966
Miscellaneous, including Profits	13%		Export		2,444
Indirect Taxes paid by purchaser	4%	49%			
	$ million				
Value of Production at ex-works price	8,310	100%			
Imports of similar goods	1,100				
Total Supply	9,410		Total Demand		9,410

Manufacture of Electrical Machinery and Equipment

INPUT			OUTPUT		
					$ *million*
Purchases of Materials, Services, Transport, etc		47%	Sales to other Industries	1,315	
			Sales to Persons	572	
			Sales to Government	—	
Value Added			Capital Formation	1,424	
Wages and Salaries	26%		Stock Variation	178	
Employers' Social Service Payments	3%				
Depreciation	3%		Apparent Consumption		3,489
Miscellaneous, including Profits	16%		Export		880
Indirect Taxes paid by purchaser	5%	53%			
	$ *million*				
Value of Production at ex-works price	4,156	100%			
Imports of similar goods	213				
Total Supply	4,369		Total Demand		4,369

Shipbuilding, Manufacture of Motor Vehicles, Motor Cycles and Cycles

INPUT			OUTPUT		
					$ *million*
Purchases of Materials, Services, Transport, etc		58%	Sales to other Industries	1,218	
			Sales to Persons	867	
			Sales to Government	—	
Value Added			Capital Formation	1,300	
Wages and Salaries	20%		Stock Variation	174	
Employers' Social Service Payments	2%				
Depreciation	4%		Apparent Consumption		3,559
Miscellaneous, including Profits	13%		Export		1,817
Indirect Taxes paid by purchaser	3%	42%			
	$ *million*				
Value of Production at ex-works price	5,155	100%			
Imports of similar goods	221				
Total Supply	5,376		Total Demand		5,376

Manufacture of Optical, Scientific and Light Engineering

INPUT			OUTPUT		
				$ *million*	
Purchases of Materials, Services, Transport, etc		49%	Sales to other Industries	410	
			Sales to Persons	675	
Value Added			Sales to Government	—	
Wages and Salaries	26%		Capital Formation	244	
Employers' Social Service Payments	3%		Stock Variation	35	
Depreciation	3%				
Miscellaneous, including Profits	15%		Apparent Consumption		1,364
Indirect Taxes paid by purchaser	4%	51%	Export		528
		$ *million*			
Value of Production at ex-works price	1,721	100%			
Imports of similar goods	171				
Total Supply	1,892		Total Demand		1,892

TABLE 3: ITALY

Manufacture of Hosiery, Knitwear and Knitted Fabrics

INPUT			OUTPUT		
					$ *million*
Purchases of Materials, Services,			Sales to other Industries		*
Transport, etc		64%	Sales to Persons ⎫	204	
			Sales to Government ⎭		
Value Added			Capital Formation		—
Wages and Salaries	18%		Stock Variation		*
Employers' Social Service Payments	6%				
Depreciation	12%		Apparent Consumption		204
Miscellaneous, including Profits	—		Export		72
Indirect Taxes paid by purchaser	—	36%			
	$ *million*				
Value of Production at ex-works price	272	100%			
Imports of similar goods	4				
Total Supply	276		Total Demand		276

* negligible

Manufacture of Wearing Apparel

INPUT			OUTPUT		
					$ *million*
Purchases of Materials, Services,			Sales to other Industries	64	
Transport, etc		65%	Sales to Persons ⎫	784	
			Sales to Government ⎭		
Value Added			Capital Formation	10	
Wages and Salaries	7%		Stock Variation	7	
Employers' Social Service Payments	2%				
Depreciation	25%		Apparent Consumption		865
Miscellaneous, including Profits	—		Export		46
Indirect Taxes paid by purchaser	1%	35%			
	$ *million*				
Value of Production at ex-works price	896	100%			
Imports of similar goods	15				
Total Supply	911		Total Demand		911

Manufacture and Repairing of Footwear

INPUT			OUTPUT		$ *million*
Purchases of Materials, Services, Transport, etc		57%	Sales to other Industries	5	
			Sales to Persons ⎱	234	
			Sales to Government ⎰		
Value Added			Capital Formation	—	
Wages and Salaries	7%		Stock Variation	—	
Employers' Social Service Payments	3%				
Depreciation	31%		Apparent Consumption		239
Miscellaneous, including Profits	—		Export		72
Indirect Taxes paid by purchaser	2%	43%			

	$ *million*	
Value of Production at ex-works price	309	100%
Imports of similar goods	2	
Total Supply	311	

Total Demand	311

Manufacture of Pulp, Paper and Paper Board

INPUT			OUTPUT		$ *million*
Purchases of Materials, Services, Transport, etc		54%	Sales to other Industries	477	
			Sales to Persons ⎱	31	
			Sales to Government ⎰		
Value Added			Capital Formation	—	
Wages and Salaries	19%		Stock Variation	—	
Employers' Social Service Payments	6%				
Depreciation	16%		Apparent Consumption		508
Miscellaneous, including Profits	—		Export		13
Indirect Taxes paid by purchaser	5%	46%			

	$ *million*	
Value of Production at ex-works price	426	100%
Imports of similar goods	95	
Total Supply	521	

Total Demand	521

Printing, Publishing and Allied Industries

INPUT			OUTPUT	
				$ million
Purchase of Materials, Services,			Sales to other Industries	314
Transport, etc		48%	Sales to Persons ⎱	
			Sales to Government ⎰	271
Value Added			Capital Formation	—
Wages and Salaries	29%		Stock Variation	—
Employers' Social Service Payments	9%			
Depreciation	12%		Apparent Consumption	585
Miscellaneous, including Profits	2%		Export	11
Indirect Taxes paid by purchaser	—	52%		
	$ million			
Value of Production at ex-works price	589	100%		
Imports of similar goods	7			
Total Supply	596		Total Demand	596

Manufacture of Leather Products, except Footwear

INPUT			OUTPUT	
				$ million
Purchases of Materials, Services,			Sales to other Industries	164
Transport, etc		70%	Sales to Persons ⎱	
			Sales to Government ⎰	100
Value Added			Capital Formation	1
Wages and Salaries	9%		Stock Variation	—3
Employers' Social Service Payments	3%			
Depreciation	15%		Apparent Consumption	262
Miscellaneous, including Profits	—		Export	21
Indirect Taxes paid by purchaser	3%	30%		
	$ million			
Value of Production at ex-works price	262	100%		
Imports of similar goods	21			
Total Supply	283		Total Demand	283

Manufacture of Rubber and Asbestos Products

INPUT			OUTPUT		
					$ *million*
Purchases of Materials, Services, Transport, etc		60%	Sales to other Industries	178	
			Sales to Persons ⎱ Sales to Government ⎰	56	
Value Added			Capital Formation	5	
Wages and Salaries	18%		Stock Variation	10	
Employers' Social Service Payments	5%				
Depreciation	14%		Apparent Consumption		249
Miscellaneous, including Profits	—		Export		19
Indirect Taxes paid by purchaser	3%	40%			
	$ *million*				
Value of Production at ex-works price	258	100%			
Imports of similar goods	10				
Total Supply	268		Total Demand		268

Manufacture of Plastic Products

INPUT			OUTPUT		
					$ *million*
Purchases of Materials, Services, Transport, etc		69%	Sales to other Industries	117	
			Sales to Persons ⎱ Sales to Government ⎰	53	
Value Added			Capital Formation	9	
Wages and Salaries	9%		Stock Variation	*	
Employers' Social Service Payments	4%				
Depreciation	14%		Apparent Consumption		179
Miscellaneous, including Profits	—		Export		10
Indirect Taxes paid by purchaser	4%	31%			
	$ *million*				
Value of Production at ex-works price	185	100%			
Imports of similar goods	4				
Total Supply	189		Total Demand		189

* negligible

Manufacture of Synthetic Materials and Fibres

INPUT			OUTPUT		
					$ million
Purchases of Materials, Services, Transport, etc		55%	Sales to other Industries	298	
			Sales to Persons ⎱	—	
			Sales to Government ⎰		
Value Added			Capital Formation	—	
Wages and Salaries	13%		Stock Variation	9	
Employers' Social Service Payments	5%				
Depreciation	24%		Apparent Consumption		307
Miscellaneous, including Profits	—		Export		118
Indirect Taxes paid by purchaser	3%	45%			
	$ million				
Value of Production at ex-works price	367	100%			
Imports of similar goods	58				
Total Supply	425		Total Demand		425

Other Basic Chemical Industries, including the production of Fertilizers

INPUT			OUTPUT		
					$ million
Purchases of Materials, Services, Transport, etc		60%	Sales to other Industries	1,056	
			Sales to Persons ⎱	358	
			Sales to Government ⎰		
Value Added			Capital Formation	—	
Wages and Salaries	13%		Stock Variation	24	
Employers' Social Service Payments	6%				
Depreciation	17%		Apparent Consumption		1,438
Miscellaneous, including Profits	—		Export		147
Indirect Taxes paid by purchaser	4%	40%			
	$ million				
Value of Production at ex-works price	1,378	100%			
Imports of similar goods	207				
Total Supply	1,585		Total Demand		1,585

Manufacture of Other Chemicals

INPUT			OUTPUT	$ *million*
Purchases of Materials, Services, Transport, etc		60%	Sales to other Industries	40
			Sales to Persons ⎫	
			Sales to Government ⎭	291
Value Added			Capital Formation	—
Wages and Salaries	15%		Stock Variation	8
Employers' Social Service Payments	4%			
Depreciation	16%		Apparent Consumption	339
Miscellaneous, including Profits	—		Export	28
Indirect Taxes paid by purchaser	5%	40%		
	$ *million*			
Value of Production at ex-works price	328	100%		
Imports of similar goods	39			
Total Supply	367		Total Demand	367

Manufacture of Glass and Glass Products

INPUT			OUTPUT	$ *million*
Purchases of Materials, Services, Transport, etc		48%	Sales to other Industries	143
			Sales to Persons ⎫	
			Sales to Government ⎭	17
Value Added			Capital Formation	20
Wages and Salaries	21%		Stock Variation	6
Employers' Social Service Payments	7%			
Depreciation	20%		Apparent Consumption	186
Miscellaneous, including Profits	—		Export	12
Indirect Taxes paid by purchaser	4%	52%		
	$ *million*			
Value of Production at ex-works price	165	100%		
Imports of similar goods	33			
Total Supply	198		Total Demand	198

Iron and Steel Basic Industries (*ECSC*)

INPUT			OUTPUT		
					$ *million*
Purchases of Materials, Services,			Sales to other Industries	866	
Transport, etc		62%	Sales to Persons ⎫		—
			Sales to Government ⎰		
Value Added			Capital Formation	5	
Wages and Salaries	12%		Stock Variation	8	
Employers' Social Service Payments	4%				
Depreciation	19%		Apparent Consumption		879
Miscellaneous, including Profits	—		Export		96
Indirect Taxes paid by purchaser	3%	38%			
	$ *million*				
Value of Production at ex-works price	815	100%			
Imports of similar goods	160				
Total Supply	975		Total Demand		975

Production and Manufactures of Non-Ferrous Metals

INPUT			OUTPUT		
					$ *million*
Purchases of Materials, Services,			Sales to other Industries	445	
Transport, etc		67%	Sales to Persons ⎫		—
			Sales to Government ⎰		
Value Added			Capital Formation		—
Wages and Salaries	14%		Stock Variation	—2	
Employers' Social Service Payments	5%				
Depreciation	10%		Apparent Consumption		443
Miscellaneous, including Profits	—		Export		37
Indirect Taxes paid by purchaser	4%	33%			
	$ *million*				
Value of Production at ex-works price	335	100%			
Imports of similar goods	145				
Total Supply	480		Total Demand		480

67

Manufacture of Metallic Products and Furniture, except Machinery

INPUT			OUTPUT		
					$ million
Purchases of Materials, Services,			Sales to other Industries	340	
Transport, etc		59%	Sales to Persons ⎫		26
			Sales to Government ⎭		
Value Added			Capital Formation	267	
Wages and Salaries	20%		Stock Variation	4	
Employers' Social Service Payments	8%				
Depreciation	12%		Apparent Consumption		637
Miscellaneous, including Profits	—		Export		81
Indirect Taxes paid by purchaser	1%	41%			
	$ million				
Value of Production at ex-works price	663	100%			
Imports of similar goods	55				
Total Supply	718		Total Demand		718

Manufacture of Agricultural Machinery and Tractors

INPUT			OUTPUT		
					$ million
Purchases of Materials, Services,			Sales to other Industries	2	
Transport, etc		71%	Sales to Persons ⎫		—
			Sales to Government ⎭		
Value Added			Capital Formation	125	
Wages and Salaries	14%		Stock Variation	5	
Employers' Social Service Payments	5%				
Depreciation	8%		Apparent Consumption		132
Miscellaneous, including Profits	—		Export		18
Indirect Taxes paid by purchaser	2%	29%			
	$ million				
Value of Production at ex-works price	129	100%			
Imports of similar goods	21				
Total Supply	150		Total Demand		150

Manufacture of other Machinery, except Electrical Machinery

INPUT			OUTPUT		
				$ *million*	
Purchases of Materials, Services,			Sales to other Industries	77	
Transport, etc		52%	Sales to Persons ⎫	25	
			Sales to Government ⎭		
Value Added			Capital Formation	734	
Wages and Salaries	21%		Stock Variation	14	
Employers' Social Service Payments	8%				
Depreciation	17%		Apparent Consumption		850
Miscellaneous, including Profits	—		Export		298
Indirect Taxes paid by purchaser	2%	48%			
	$ *million*				
Value of Production at ex-works price	865	100%			
Imports of similar goods	283				
Total Supply	1,148		Total Demand		1,148

Manufacture of Electrical Machinery and Equipment

INPUT			OUTPUT		
				$ *million*	
Purchases of Materials, Services,			Sales to other Industries	328	
Transport, etc		53%	Sales to Persons ⎫	163	
			Sales to Government ⎭		
Value Added			Capital Formation	386	
Wages and Salaries	21%		Stock Variation	21	
Employers' Social Service Payments	9%				
Depreciation	14%		Apparent Consumption		898
Miscellaneous, including Profits	—		Export		78
Indirect Taxes paid by purchaser	3%	47%			
	$ *million*				
Value of Production at ex-works price	857	100%			
Imports of similar goods	119				
Total Supply	976		Total Demand		976

Manufacture and Assembly of Motor Vehicles

INPUT			OUTPUT	
				$ *million*
Purchases of Materials, Services,			Sales to other Industries	61
Transport, etc		63%	Sales to Persons	140
			Sales to Government	
Value Added			Capital Formation	363
Wages and Salaries	19%		Stock Variation	3
Employers' Social Service Payments	6%			
Depreciation	12%		Apparent Consumption	567
Miscellaneous, including Profits	—		Export	230
Indirect Taxes paid by purchaser	—	37%		
	$ *million*			
Value of Production at ex-works price	750	100%		
Imports of similar goods	47			
Total Supply	797		Total Demand	797

TABLE 4: THE NETHERLANDS

Manufacture of Hosiery, Knitwear and Knitted Fabrics

INPUT			OUTPUT	
				$ million
Purchases of Materials, Services,			Sales to other Industries	4
Transport, etc		65%	Sales to Persons	94
			Sales to Government	—
Value Added			Capital Formation	—
Wages and Salaries	20%		Stock Variation	1
Employers' Social Service Payments	3%			
Depreciation	5%		Apparent Consumption	99
Miscellaneous, including Profits	7%		Export	15
Indirect Taxes paid by purchaser	—	35%		
	$ million			
Value of Production at ex-works price	77	100%		
Imports of similar goods	37			
Total Supply	114		Total Demand	114

Manufacture of Wearing Apparel

INPUT			OUTPUT	
				$ million
Purchases of Materials, Services,			Sales to other Industries	6
Transport, etc		62%	Sales to Persons	298
			Sales to Government	—
Value Added			Capital Formation	—
Wages and Salaries	22%		Stock Variation	5
Employers' Social Service Payments	3%			
Depreciation	2%		Apparent Consumption	309
Miscellaneous, including Profits	10%		Export	34
Indirect Taxes paid by purchaser	1%	38%		
	$ million			
Value of Production at ex-works price	306	100%		
Imports of similar goods	37			
Total Supply	343		Total Demand	343

Manufacture of Made-up Textile Goods, except Wearing Apparel

INPUT			OUTPUT		
					$ million
Purchases of Materials, Services, Transport, etc		67%	Sales to other Industries	18	
			Sales to Persons	35	
			Sales to Government	3	
Value Added			Capital Formation	—	
Wages and Salaries	21%		Stock Variation	1	
Employers' Social Service Payments	3%				
Depreciation	2%		Apparent Consumption		57
Miscellaneous, including Profits	6%		Export		4
Indirect Taxes paid by purchaser	1%	33%			
	$ million				
Value of Production at ex-works price	46	100%			
Imports of similar goods	15				
Total Supply	61		Total Demand		61

Manufacture and Repairing of Footwear

INPUT			OUTPUT		
					$ million
Purchases of Materials, Services, Transport, etc		55%	Sales to other Industries	—	
			Sales to Persons	94	
			Sales to Government	—	
Value Added			Capital Formation	—	
Wages and Salaries	22%		Stock Variation	9	
Employers' Social Service Payments	3%				
Depreciation	3%		Apparent Consumption		103
Miscellaneous, including Profits	17%		Export		11
Indirect Taxes paid by purchaser	—	45%			
	$ million				
Value of Production at ex-works price	105	100%			
Imports of similar goods	9				
Total Supply	114		Total Demand		114

Manufacture of Rubber and Asbestos Products

INPUT			OUTPUT		
				$ *million*	
Purchases of Materials, Services,			Sales to other Industries	63	
Transport, etc		63%	Sales to Persons	12	
			Sales to Government	2	
Value Added			Capital Formation	1	
Wages and Salaries	18%		Stock Variation	3	
Employers' Social Service Payments	3%				
Depreciation	2%		Apparent Consumption		81
Miscellaneous, including Profits	8%		Export		25
Indirect Taxes paid by purchaser	6%	37%			
	$ *million*				
Value of Production at ex-works price	76	100%			
Imports of similar goods	30				
Total Supply	106		Total Demand		106

Manufacture of Plastic Products

INPUT			OUTPUT		
				$ *million*	
Purchases of Materials, Services,			Sales to other Industries	107	
Transport, etc		59%	Sales to Persons	8	
			Sales to Government	—	
Value Added			Capital Formation	—	
Wages and Salaries	19%		Stock Variation	−2	
Employers' Social Service Payments	4%				
Depreciation	8%		Apparent Consumption		113
Miscellaneous, including Profits	8%		Export		97
Indirect Taxes paid by purchaser	2%	41%			
	$ *million*				
Value of Production at ex-works price	144	100%			
Imports of similar goods	66				
Total Supply	210		Total Demand		210

Other Basic Chemical Industries, including the production of Fertilizers

INPUT			OUTPUT		
					$ million
Purchases of Materials, Services,			Sales to other Industries	284	
Transport, etc		68%	Sales to Persons	3	
			Sales to Government	4	
Value Added			Capital Formation	5	
Wages and Salaries	10%		Stock Variation	2	
Employers' Social Service Payments	2%				
Depreciation	6%		Apparent Consumption		298
Miscellaneous, including Profits	11%		Export		150
Indirect Taxes paid by purchaser	3%	32%			
	$ million				
Value of Production at ex-works price	311	100%			
Imports of similar goods	137				
Total Supply	448		Total Demand		448

Manufacture of Chemicals

INPUT			OUTPUT		
					$ million
Purchases of Materials, Services,			Sales to other Industries	142	
Transport, etc		60%	Sales to Persons	102	
			Sales to Government	6	
Value Added			Capital Formation	—	
Wages and Salaries	15%		Stock Variation	2	
Employers' Social Service Payments	2%				
Depreciation	5%		Apparent Consumption		252
Miscellaneous, including Profits	15%		Export		102
Indirect Taxes paid by purchaser	3%	40%			
	$ million				
Value of Production at ex-works price	264	100%			
Imports of similar goods	90				
Total Supply	354		Total Demand		354

Manufacture of Glass and Glass Products

INPUT			OUTPUT	
				$ *million*
Purchases of Materials, Services, Transport, etc		41%	Sales to other Industries	45
			Sales to Persons	11
			Sales to Government	—
Value Added			Capital Formation	1
Wages and Salaries	32%		Stock Variation	1
Employers' Social Service Payments	5%			
Depreciation	4%		Apparent Consumption	58
Miscellaneous, including Profits	14%		Export	3
Indirect Taxes paid by purchaser	4%	59%		
		$ *million*		
Value of Production at ex-works price	21	100%		
Imports of similar goods	40			
Total Supply	61		Total Demand	61

Iron and Steel Basic Industries (*ECSC*)

INPUT			OUTPUT	
				$ *million*
Purchases of Materials, Services, Transport, etc		58%	Sales to other Industries	416
			Sales to Persons	—
			Sales to Government	—
Value Added			Capital Formation	19
Wages and Salaries	11%		Stock Variation	2
Employers' Social Service Payments	1%			
Depreciation	5%		Apparent Consumption	437
Miscellaneous, including Profits	20%		Export	148
Indirect Taxes paid by purchaser	5%	42%		
		$ *million*		
Value of Production at ex-works price	313	100%		
Imports of similar goods	272			
Total Supply	585		Total Demand	585

Production and Manufactures of Non-Ferrous Metals

INPUT			OUTPUT		
					$ million
Purchases of Materials, Services, Transport, etc		87%	Sales to other Industries	179	
			Sales to Persons	3	
			Sales to Government	2	
Value Added			Capital Formation	—	
Wages and Salaries	6%		Stock Variation	—3	
Employers' Social Service Payments	1%				
Depreciation	1%		Apparent Consumption		181
Miscellaneous, including Profits	4%		Export		79
Indirect Taxes paid by purchaser	1%	13%			
	$ million				
Value of Production at ex-works price	122	100%			
Imports of similar goods	138				
Total Supply	260		Total Demand		260

Manufacture of Metallic Products and Furniture, except Machinery

INPUT			OUTPUT		
					$ million
Purchases of Materials, Services, Transport, etc		59%	Sales to other Industries	306	
			Sales to Persons	81	
			Sales to Government	5	
Value Added			Capital Formation	76	
Wages and Salaries	21%		Stock Variation	4	
Employers' Social Service Payments	3%				
Depreciation	2%		Apparent Consumption		472
Miscellaneous, including Profits	10%		Export		83
Indirect Taxes paid by purchaser	5%	41%			
	$ million				
Value of Production at ex-works price	459	100%			
Imports of similar goods	96				
Total Supply	555		Total Demand		555

Manufacture of Agricultural Machinery and Tractors, and other Machinery except Electrical

INPUT			OUTPUT	
				$ million
Purchases of Materials, Services, Transport, etc		52%	Sales to other Industries	234
			Sales to Persons	25
			Sales to Government	13
Value Added			Capital Formation	320
Wages and Salaries	26%		Stock Variation	4
Employers' Social Service Payments	4%			
Depreciation	3%		Apparent Consumption	596
Miscellaneous, including Profits	12%		Export	156
Indirect Taxes paid by purchaser	3%	48%		
	$ million			
Value of Production at ex-works price	384	100%		
Imports of similar goods	368			
Total Supply	752		Total Demand	752

Manufacture of Electrical Machinery and Equipment

INPUT			OUTPUT	
				$ million
Purchases of Materials, Services, Transport, etc		46%	Sales to other Industries	262
			Sales to Persons	103
			Sales to Government	6
Value Added			Capital Formation	142
Wages and Salaries	23%		Stock Variation	13
Employers' Social Service Payments	3%			
Depreciation	3%		Apparent Consumption	526
Miscellaneous, including Profits	22%		Export	356
Indirect Taxes paid by purchaser	3%	54%		
	$ million			
Value of Production at ex-works price	612	100%		
Imports of similar goods	270			
Total Supply	882		Total Demand	882

Manufacture and Assembly of Motor Vehicles

INPUT			OUTPUT		
					$ million
Purchases of Materials, Services, Transport, etc		67%	Sales to other Industries	66	
			Sales to Persons	17	
			Sales to Government	15	
Value Added			Capital Formation	161	
Wages and Salaries	14%		Stock Variation	4	
Employers' Social Service Payments	3%				
Depreciation	3%		Apparent Consumption		263
Miscellaneous, including Profits	7%		Export		24
Indirect Taxes paid by purchaser	6%	33%			
	$ million				
Value of Production at ex-works price	118	100%			
Imports of similar goods	169				
Total Supply	287		Total Demand		287

Manufacture of Professional, Scientific, Measuring and Control Instruments; Photographic and Optical Goods; Watches and Clocks, Jewellery, Musical Instruments, and Toys

INPUT			OUTPUT		
					$ million
Purchases of Materials, Services, Transport, etc		59%	Sales to other Industries	159	
			Sales to Persons	65	
			Sales to Government	10	
Value Added			Capital Formation	50	
Wages and Salaries	22%		Stock Variation	1	
Employers' Social Service Payments	3%				
Depreciation	2%		Apparent Consumption		285
Miscellaneous, including Profits	11%		Export		67
Indirect Taxes paid by purchaser	3%	41%			
	$ million				
Value of Production at ex-works price	278	100%			
Imports of similar goods	74				
Total Supply	352		Total Demand		352

Manufacture of Hosiery, Knitwear and Knitted Fabrics

INPUT			OUTPUT	
				$ million
Purchases of Materials, Services, Transport, etc		56%	Sales to other Industries	1
			Sales to Persons	76
			Sales to Government	—
Value Added			Capital Formation	—
Wages and Salaries	21%		Stock Variation	2
Employers' Social Service Payments	4%			
Depreciation	5%		Apparent Consumption	79
Miscellaneous, including Profits	8%		Export	27
Indirect Taxes paid by purchaser	6%	44%		
	$ million			
Value of Production at ex-works price	87	100%		
Imports of similar goods	19			
Total Supply	106		Total Demand	106

Manufacture of Wearing Apparel

INPUT			OUTPUT	
				$ million
Purchases of Materials, Services, Transport, etc		60%	Sales to other Industries	1
			Sales to Persons	261
			Sales to Government	2
Value Added			Capital Formation	—
Wages and Salaries	18%		Stock Variation	2
Employers' Social Service Payments	3%			
Depreciation	2%		Apparent Consumption	266
Miscellaneous, including Profits	12%		Export	43
Indirect Taxes paid by purchaser	4%	39%		
	$ million			
Value of Production at ex-works price	272	100%		
Imports of similar goods	37			
Total Supply	309		Total Demand	309

Manufacture and Repairing of Footwear

INPUT			OUTPUT	
				$ *million*
Purchases of Materials, Services,			Sales to other Industries	2
Transport, etc		49%	Sales to Persons	84
			Sales to Government	*
Value Added			Capital Formation	*
Wages and Salaries	22%		Stock Variation	1
Employers' Social Service Payments	4%			
Depreciation	2%		Apparent Consumption	87
Miscellaneous, including Profits	20%		Export	10
Indirect Taxes paid by purchaser	3%	51%		
	$ *million*			
Value of Production at ex-works price	81	100%		
Imports of similar goods	16			
Total Supply	97		Total Demand	97
			* negligible	

Manufacture of Pulp, Paper and Paper Board

INPUT			OUTPUT	
				$ *million*
Purchases of Materials, Services,			Sales to other Industries	194
Transport, etc		54%	Sales to Persons	12
			Sales to Government	4
Value Added			Capital Formation	*
Wages and Salaries	23%		Stock Variation	−1
Employers' Social Service Payments	4%			
Depreciation	8%		Apparent Consumption	209
Miscellaneous, including Profits	6%		Export	34
Indirect Taxes paid by purchaser	5%	46%		
	$ *million*			
Value of Production at ex-works price	152	100%		
Imports of similar goods	91			
Total Supply	243		Total Demand	243
			* negligible	

Printing, Publishing and Allied Industries

INPUT			OUTPUT		
					$ *million*
Purchases of Materials, Services, Transport, etc		44%	Sales to other Industries	116	
			Sales to Persons	33	
			Sales to Government	14	
Value Added			Capital Formation	—	
Wages and Salaries	30%		Stock Variation	—	
Employers' Social Service Payments	5%				
Depreciation	7%		Apparent Consumption		163
Miscellaneous, including Profits	11%		Export		21
Indirect Taxes paid by purchaser	3%	56%			
	$ *million*				
Value of Production at ex-works price	155	100%			
Imports of similar goods	29				
Total Supply	184		Total Demand		184

Manufacture of Leather Products, except Footwear

INPUT			OUTPUT		
					$ *million*
Purchases of Materials, Services, Transport, etc		63%	Sales to other Industries	44	
			Sales to Persons	10	
			Sales to Government	*	
Value Added			Capital Formation	*	
Wages and Salaries	22%		Stock Variation	*	
Employers' Social Service Payments	3%				
Depreciation	2%		Apparent Consumption		54
Miscellaneous, including Profits	6%		Export		15
Indirect Taxes paid by purchaser	4%	37%			
	$ *million*				
Value of Production at ex-works price	44	100%			
Imports of similar goods	25				
Total Supply	69		Total Demand		69

* negligible

Manufacture of Rubber and Asbestos Products

INPUT			OUTPUT	
				$ *million*
Purchases of Materials, Services, Transport, etc		60%	Sales to other Industries	68
			Sales to Persons	2
			Sales to Government	1
Value Added			Capital Formation	—
Wages and Salaries	28%		Stock Variation	1
Employers' Social Service Payments	3%			
Depreciation	4%		Apparent Consumption	72
Miscellaneous, including Profits	1%		Export	13
Indirect Taxes paid by purchaser	4%	40%		
	$ *million*			
Value of Production at ex-works price	50	100%		
Imports of similar goods	35			
Total Supply	85		Total Demand	85

Manufacture of Plastic Products

INPUT			OUTPUT	
				$ *million*
Purchases of Materials, Services, Transport, etc		57%	Sales to other Industries	24
			Sales to Persons	8
			Sales to Government	*
Value Added			Capital Formation	—
Wages and Salaries	24%		Stock Variation	—
Employers' Social Service Payments	3%			
Depreciation	5%		Apparent Consumption	32
Miscellaneous, including Profits	6%		Export	5
Indirect Taxes paid by purchaser	5%	43%		
	$ *million*			
Value of Production at ex-works price	22	100%		
Imports of similar goods	15			
Total Supply	37		Total Demand	37

* negligible

Other Basic Chemical Industries, including the production of Fertilizers

INPUT			OUTPUT		
					$ *million*
Purchases of Materials, Services,			Sales to other Industries	203	
Transport, etc		62%	Sales to Persons	2	
			Sales to Government	5	
Value Added			Capital Formation	3	
Wages and Salaries	21%		Stock Variation	6	
Employers' Social Service Payments	2%				
Depreciation	10%		Apparent Consumption		219
Miscellaneous, including Profits	3%		Export		140
Indirect Taxes paid by purchaser	2%	38%			
		$ *million*			
Value of Production at ex-works price	208	100%			
Imports of similar goods	151				
Total Supply	359		Total Demand		359

Manufacture of Synthetic Materials and Fibres

INPUT			OUTPUT		
					$ *million*
Purchases of Materials, Services,			Sales to other Industries	79	
Transport, etc		60%	Sales to Persons	—	
			Sales to Government	1	
Value Added			Capital Formation	—	
Wages and Salaries	20%		Stock Variation	1	
Employers' Social Service Payments	2%				
Depreciation	10%		Apparent Consumption		81
Miscellaneous, including Profits	6%		Export		35
Indirect Taxes paid by purchaser	2%	40%			
		$ *million*			
Value of Production at ex-works price	57	100%			
Imports of similar goods	59				
Total Supply	116		Total Demand		116

Manufacture of Soaps, Detergents, Perfumes, etc.

INPUT			OUTPUT	
				$ *million*
Purchases of Materials, Services, Transport, etc		64%	Sales to other Industries	13
			Sales to Persons	49
			Sales to Government	2
Value Added			Capital Formation	—
Wages and Salaries	15%		Stock Variation	—1
Employers' Social Service Payments	1%			
Depreciation	4%		Apparent Consumption	63
Miscellaneous, including Profits	11%		Export	12
Indirect Taxes paid by purchaser	5%	36%		
	$ *million*			
Value of Production at ex-works price	60	100%		
Imports of similar goods	15			
Total Supply	75		Total Demand	75

Manufacture of Glass and Glass Products

INPUT			OUTPUT	
				$ *million*
Purchases of Materials, Services, Transport, etc		42%	Sales to other Industries	23
			Sales to Persons	8
			Sales to Government	1
Value Added			Capital Formation	—
Wages and Salaries	34%		Stock Variation	—3
Employers' Social Service Payments	5%			
Depreciation	7%		Apparent Consumption	29
Miscellaneous, including Profits	10%		Export	98
Indirect Taxes paid by purchaser	2%	58%		
	$ *million*			
Value of Production at ex-works price	114	100%		
Imports of similar goods	13			
Total Supply	127		Total Demand	127

Iron and Steel Basic Industries (ECSC) Blast Furnaces

INPUT			OUTPUT	$ million
Purchases of Materials, Services, Transport, etc		86%	Sales to other Industries	296
			Sales to Persons	—
			Sales to Government	*
Value Added			Capital Formation	—
Wages and Salaries	8%		Stock Variation	2
Employers' Social Service Payments	1%			
Depreciation	4%		Apparent Consumption	298
Miscellaneous, including Profits	1%		Export	7
Indirect Taxes paid by purchaser	—	14%		
	$ million			
Value of Production at ex-works price	290	100%		
Imports of similar goods	15			
Total Supply	305		Total Demand	305

* negligible

Steel Manufactures

INPUT			OUTPUT	$ million
Purchases of Materials, Services, Transport, etc		90%	Sales to other Industries	420
			Sales to Persons	—
			Sales to Government	—
Value Added			Capital Formation	*
Wages and Salaries	6%		Stock Variation	*
Employers' Social Service Payments	1%			
Depreciation	2%		Apparent Consumption	420
Miscellaneous, including Profits	1%		Export	12
Indirect Taxes paid by purchaser	—	10%		
	$ million			
Value of Production at ex-works price	431	100%		
Imports of similar goods	1			
Total Supply	432		Total Demand	432

* negligible

Rolling Mills

INPUT			OUTPUT		
				$ *million*	
Purchases of Materials, Services, Transport, etc		80%	Sales to other Industries	300	
			Sales to Persons	—	
			Sales to Government	*	
Value Added			Capital Formation	1	
Wages and Salaries	11%		Stock Variation	2	
Employers' Social Service Payments	2%				
Depreciation	4%		Apparent Consumption		303
Miscellaneous, including Profits	2%		Export		432
Indirect Taxes paid by purchaser	1%	20%			
	$ *million*				
Value of Production at ex-works price	625	100%			
Imports of similar goods	110				
Total Supply	735		Total Demand		735

* negligible

Manufacture of Metal Products and Furniture, except Machinery

INPUT			OUTPUT		
				$ *million*	
Purchases of Materials, Services, Transport, etc		58%	Sales to other Industries	183	
			Sales to Persons	82	
			Sales to Government	5	
Value Added			Capital Formation	33	
Wages and Salaries	28%		Stock Variation	—	
Employers' Social Service Payments	5%				
Depreciation	4%		Apparent Consumption		303
Miscellaneous, including Profits	2%		Export		84
Indirect Taxes paid by purchaser	3%	42%			
	$ *million*				
Value of Production at ex-works price	312	100%			
Imports of similar goods	75				
Total Supply	387		Total Demand		387

Manufacture of Agricultural Machinery and Tractors

INPUT			OUTPUT		
				$ *million*	
Purchases of Materials, Services,			Sales to other Industries	6	
Transport, etc		48%	Sales to Persons	—	
			Sales to Government	—	
Value Added			Capital Formation	24	
Wages and Salaries	24%		Stock Variation	*	
Employers' Social Service Payments	4%				
Depreciation	4%		Apparent Consumption		30
Miscellaneous, including Profits	17%		Export		10
Indirect Taxes paid by purchaser	3%	52%			
	$ *million*				
Value of Production at ex-works price	22	100%			
Imports of similar goods	18				
Total Supply	40		Total Demand		40

* negligible

Manufacture of Other Machinery, except Electrical Machinery

INPUT			OUTPUT		
				$ *million*	
Purchases of Materials, Services,			Sales to other Industries	157	
Transport, etc		46%	Sales to Persons	49	
			Sales to Government	21	
Value Added			Capital Formation	236	
Wages and Salaries	32%		Stock Variation	8	
Employers' Social Service Payments	5%				
Depreciation	5%		Apparent Consumption		471
Miscellaneous, including Profits	10%		Export		159
Indirect Taxes paid by purchaser	2%	54%			
	$ *million*				
Value of Production at ex-works price	360	100%			
Imports of similar goods	270				
Total Supply	630		Total Demand		630

Manufacture of Electrical Machinery and Equipment

INPUT			OUTPUT		
					$ *million*
Purchases of Materials, Services, Transport, etc		47%	Sales to other Industries	91	
			Sales to Persons	60	
			Sales to Government	7	
Value Added			Capital Formation	127	
Wages and Salaries	34%		Stock Variation	−1	
Employers' Social Service Payments	5%				
Depreciation	5%		Apparent Consumption		284
Miscellaneous, including Profits	6%		Export		95
Indirect Taxes paid by purchaser	3%	53%			
	$ *million*				
Value of Production at ex-works price	244	100%			
Imports of similar goods	135				
Total Supply	379		Total Demand		379

Manufacture and Assembly of Motor Vehicles

INPUT			OUTPUT		
					$ *million*
Purchases of Materials, Services, Transport, etc		78%	Sales to other Industries	180	
			Sales to Persons	96	
			Sales to Government	*	
Value Added			Capital Formation	117	
Wages and Salaries	11%		Stock Variation	−6	
Employers' Social Service Payments	1%				
Depreciation	3%		Apparent Consumption		387
Miscellaneous, including Profits	4%		Export		85
Indirect Taxes paid by purchaser	3%	22%			
	$ *million*				
Value of Production at ex-works price	255	100%			
Imports of similar goods	217				
Total Supply	472		Total Demand		472

* negligible

Manufacture of Professional, Scientific, Measuring and Control Instruments; Photographic and Optical Goods; Watches and Clocks

INPUT			OUTPUT	
				$ *million*
Purchases of Materials, Services,			Sales to other Industries	4
Transport, etc		46%	Sales to Persons	14
			Sales to Government	1
Value Added			Capital Formation	27
Wages and Salaries	27%		Stock Variation	*
Employers' Social Service Payments	5%			
Depreciation	3%		Apparent Consumption	46
Miscellaneous, including Profits	16%		Export	5
Indirect Taxes paid by purchaser	3%	54%		
	$ *million*			
Value of Production at ex-works price	13	100%		
Imports of similar goods	38			
Total Supply	51		Total Demand	51
			* negligible	

89

PART III

Production figures for some fifty basic commodities in the Common Market, together with each country's share of the total figures.

PREFACE

These production figures are for 1962, and, again, approximation has been inevitable in some instances. Some details are not available at all, but they do give, however, a very real picture of the industrial scene in the Common Market countries. Exporters and potential investors in any of the fifty or so manufactures listed can easily determine where their best markets lie if they consider the following table together with the statistical information in Parts I, II and IV.

INDEX

page

BASE METALS   93
Iron and Steel Products, Non-ferrous Metal Products

CHEMICALS   93

HOUSEHOLD AND CONSUMER DURABLES   94

OFFICE EQUIPMENT   94

PRODUCTION MACHINERY   93, 94

PULP AND PAPER   93

RUBBER MANUFACTURES   94
Tyres

TEXTILES AND CLOTHING   94

TRANSPORT   94
Automobiles, Tractors

Product Group	Total Production (*Approx.*)	Unit	Per Cent in each Common Market Country				
			France	Germany	Nether-lands	Belgium/Lux.	Italy
IRON AND STEEL							
Blooms, Billets, etc	3,248	'000 tons	11%	56%	1%	7%	25%
Angles, Shapes and Sections, heavy	4,500	,,	20%	46%	—	21%	13%
Bars and Rods for Tube manufacture	1,830	,,	23%	61%	—	neg	16%
Wire Rod	5,223	,,	30%	40%	2%	17%	11%
Hot-rolled and cold-rolled Sheets and Plates 3 mm and over	7,369	,,	18%	53%	6%	10%	13%
Cold-rolled Sheets, under 3 mm	8,786	,,	33%	27%	10%	15%	15%
Tinplate	2,580	,,	37%	26%	8%	19%	10%
Steel Tube, welded	2,652	,,	24%	49%	na†	9%	18%
Steel Tube, weldless	2,688	,,	17%	51%	na	2%	30%
Bolts and Nuts	586	,,	25%	56%	5%	9%	4%
NON-FERROUS METALS							
Zinc, worked	200	,,	35%	38%	na	22%	5%
Aluminium, worked	579	,,	27%	43%	na	14%	16%
Copper	1,319	,,	25%	44%	na	9%	22%
of which:							
Wire	540	,,	29%	46%	na	na	25%
Lead, worked	175	,,	25%	27%	10%	16%	22%
CHEMICAL PRODUCTS							
Paints and Varnishes	1,419	,,	33%	41%	8%	5%	13%
Soaps	647	,,	30%	18%	9%	7%	35%
Surface-acting preparations	880	,,	33%	36%	5%	6%	20%
PULP AND PAPER							
Paper Pulp	3,489	,,	35%	40%	4%	5%	16%
Paper	9,315	,,	30%	39%	7%	5%	19%
PRODUCTION MACHINERY							
Metal-working Machine Tools	546	,,	14%	67%	1%	2%	16%
Wood-working Machinery	89	,,	10%	77%	2%	5%	6%
Iron and Steel Plant	285	,,	18%	63%	na	7%	12%
Mining Machinery	333	,,	22%	74%	na	4%	na
Road-making Machinery	525	,,	24%	60%	na	3%	13%
Cement and Brickmaking Machinery	193	,,	31%	64%	na	6%	*

* Included in preceding heading.   † na—not available.

Product Group	Total Production (*Approx.*)	Unit	Per Cent in each Common Market Country				
			France	Germany	Netherlands	Belgium/Lux.	Italy
Machinery for Chemical Industries	141	'000 tons	14%	63%	na†	5%	18%
Rubber and Plastic-making Machinery	60	,,	12%	87%	na	1%	na
Paper and Pulp M/c	132	,,	15%	80%	na	2%	4%
Printing Machinery	65	,,	9%	91%	na	na	na
Food Processing M/c	245	,,	20%	65%	na	7%	8%
Textile Machinery	274	,,	15%	45%	na	10%	30%
Lifting and Handling Machinery	677	,,	29%	55%	1%	5%	10%
Ball Bearings	124	,,	18%	62%	na	na	20%
Refractory Materials	3,665	,,	16%	67%	na	5%	12%
TRANSPORT EQUIPMENT							
Motor Cars	4,282	'000 units	29%	46%	1%	5%	19%
Tractors (Agricultural)	217	,,	27%	50%	—	—	23%
OFFICE EQUIPMENT							
Typewriters	1,850	,,	9%	55%	na	na	36%
TEXTILES AND CLOTHING							
Wool Yarn	551	'000 tons	26%	21%	5%	11%	37%
Wool Textiles	266	,,	26%	24%	10%	6%	33%
Cotton Yarn	1,108	,,	27%	34%	6%	10%	22%
Cotton Textiles	855	,,	26%	31%	10%	9%	23%
Man-made Fibres, Synthetic	246	,,	26%	38%	7%	2%	26%
—do.— Cellulose	642	,,	19%	38%	7%	6%	29%
Linen Yarn	58	,,	49%	16%	na	24%	10%
Linen Textiles	105	,,	27%	50%	1%	8%	13%
Stockings and Socks	1,290	{ million pairs	25%	43%	5%	4%	23%
Shoes	534	{ million pairs	36%	30%	6%	5%	22%
HOUSEHOLD AND CONSUMER DURABLES							
Carpets, Wool	81	'000 tons	11%	41%	16%	24%	7%
Refrigerators	4,250	'000 units	18%	38%	na	2%	42%
Sewing Machines	1,242	,,	13%	52%	na	na	35%
Electric Washing Machines	2,540	,,	24%	44%	7%	5%	20%
RUBBER MANUFACTURES							
Tyres	717	'000 tons	37%	34%	—	10%*	19%

* Includes the Netherlands.   † na—not available.

94

PART IV

Supplementary notes on production, consumption, imports and exports in Common Market countries for important commodities.

PREFACE

The emphasis in the tables presented in this book has been upon the degree of activity in relation to production, consumption, exports and imports of the individual countries of the Common Market. However, as the process of economic and political integration within the Six proceeds, the separate countries will assume the roles of zones of industrial activity rather than of national entities. With the economies of scale which will result from a domestic market of 175 million people and with the process of harmonizing and equalizing turnover taxes, social charges, transport and production and other costs, changes in the structure of the Common Market industries will undoubtedly evolve. In many industries these changes will diminish the importance of one country in the Common Market. Where an industry has hitherto enjoyed a substantial degree of protection against some of its more efficient competitors, the changes will favour the same industry in another country. This is true, also, of many agricultural products as the common agricultural policy of the European Economic Community becomes established. How far and how fast these changes will occur is, of course, difficult to estimate. National and regional traditions, both in industry and agriculture, die hard and the evolution will be slow.

The following pages set out, for a number of the more important Common Market industries, tables and notes on the structure of some industries, based on the latest information available, mainly 1963.

INDEX

	page
AUTOMOBILES	97
AUTOMOBILE ACCESSORIES	98
CONSUMER DURABLES	106
KNITWEAR	109
LEATHER FOOTWEAR	107
NON-FERROUS METALS Aluminium, Copper	98–101
OFFICE MACHINERY	106
PLASTICS	102, 103
PULP AND PAPER	104, 105
RADIO AND TELEVISION	106
STOCKINGS	108

(1) AUTOMOBILES

Production

The Common Market as a whole produced in 1963 approximately:

Private Motor Cars	4,500,000
Commercial Vehicles	525,000

Italy Fiat produces 88 per cent of the country's production of private motor cars.

France Renault, Citroen-Panhard, Simca and Peugeot produce 96 per cent between them of the country's production of private motor cars.

Germany Volkswagen, Opel, Daimler-Benz Auto-Union Group and Ford produce 89 per cent of the country's production of private motor cars.

Belgium Produces 250,000 vehicles from parts originating in other Common Market countries.

The Netherlands Has only one make of car, the DAF, which commenced production in 1959.

Exports and Imports

In 1963, *excluding all intra-Community trade*, trade with Associated Overseas Territories of the EEC and with Communist countries, the Common Market exported 978,000 cars and imported 87,000 cars, an Export:Import Ratio of about 11:1.

Of the Common Market Exports:

UK bought 45,000 cars

US bought 361,000 cars

Of the Common Market Imports:

UK supplied 75,358 cars

US supplied 6,503 cars

Relation of Exports to Production

	Total Exports as % of Production	Intra-Community Exports as % of Production	Exports to Non-Member Countries as % of Production
Germany	48%	10%	38%
France	37%	15%	22%
Italy	31%	18%	13%

(2) MOTOR CAR ACCESSORIES

The following Table shows the value of the imports of Automobile Accessories in each of the Common Market countries with the percentage shares of their principal suppliers. The figures exclude chassis. They reflect the large motor car assembly industry in Belgium which now produces about 250,000 automobiles from parts originating mainly in other Common Market countries.

| | Total Imports $ million | Percentage from Principal Suppliers | | |
		Other Common Market Countries	UK	USA
France	27	59%	15.5%	22%
Belgium/Luxembourg	259	75.5%	12%	8.5%
Netherlands	58	50%	29%	8.6%
Germany	37	65%	8%	16%
Italy	42	60%	36%	3%

(3) SOME NON-FERROUS METALS

ALUMINIUM (Primary Metal)

Production, Imports, Exports and Consumption, 1963
'000 tons

Common Market Countries

| | Production | Imports | | Exports | | Actual Consumption 1963 (Note) |
		incl. EEC	excl. EEC	incl. EEC	excl. EEC	
France	298.4	55.8	55.5	124.7	40.8	242.5
Germany	208.8	105.9	101.8	9.7	7.2	303.4
Italy	91.4	54.1	50.1	0.2	—	128.0
Netherlands	—	14.1	7.3	0.2	—	20.7*
Belgium/ Luxembourg	—	89.0	17.1	—	—	88.9

Comparison with other Countries

	Production	Imports	Exports	Consumption
UK	31.1	270.6	—	318.5
Norway	218.6	1.5	207.6	21.5
US	2,098.9	377.0	150.0	2,362.0
Canada	650.0	1.4	576.2	145.0

NOTE. The consumption figures are for actual quantities used during the year and vary slightly from Production plus Imports minus Exports.

* 1963 figures not available. The figure given is for 1962.

continued—

Common Market Imports of Aluminium come mainly from the following sources:

France	Cameroons	81%
	US and Canada	16%
Germany	EFTA (Norway, Switzerland)	55%
	US and Canada	40%
Italy	EFTA	34%
	US and Canada	44%
Netherlands	EEC (mainly France)	48%
	US and Canada	21%
	USSR	17%
Belgium/Luxembourg	EEC (mainly France)	81%
	US and Canada	9%
	USSR, etc.	7%
	EFTA	3%
UK	EFTA (Norway, Switzerland)	19%
	US and Canada	73%
	USSR	5%

Uses to which Aluminium is put in the Common Market Countries, with comparative figures for the US and UK, 1963

'000 tons

	France	Germany	Italy	Netherlands (1962)	Belgium/ Luxembourg	US	UK
Vehicle and Transport Equipment	95.4	108.0	77.0	3.0	2.2	719.3	112.5
Mechanical Engineering	23.4	42.5	14.0	4.0	1.8	176.9	23.6
Electrical Engineering	29.0	63.4	12.5	3.0	0.9	305.2	43.1
Building	18.0	28.1	22.0	5.6	5.5	686.2	29.2
Chemicals, Food and Agricultural Equipment	5.7	12.9	2.5	0.3	0.7	43.0	7.5
Packaging	24.3	39.2	18.0	6.2	3.4	226.3	27.3
Domestic and Office Appliances	28.7	13.7	14.0	6.5	2.1	243.0	42.5
Powder	7.9	3.7	1.2	0.5	neg	18.2	5.0
Iron and Steel and other Metal Industries	9.2	18.6	3.8	0.2	neg	115.2	12.4
Metal Industries n.e.s.	5.8	18.8	14.3	3.7	0.3	—	9.7
Miscellaneous	13.9	17.4	—	—	3.9	167.8	36.5
Direct Exports	36.0	51.0	8.7	8.0	68.0	213.2	55.7
Total:	297.3	417.3	188.0	41.0	89.0	2,914.3	405.0

continued—

COPPER

The following table shows, for each of the Common Market countries, as well as for Britain and the United States, Production, Import, Export and Consumption figures for Blister and Refined Copper for 1963.

'000 metric tons

	Production	Imports		Exports		Consump-tion
		Total	EEC	Total	EEC	
Germany	303	377	53	73	12	494
Benelux	271	280	17	248	174	60
Netherlands	—	26	17	1	1	26
France	34	202	79	13	12	250
Italy	13	225	25	—	—	228
Total Common Market	621	1,110	191	335	199	1,058
UK	215	501	—	87	62	558
US	1,710	442	—	282	159	1,593

The breakdown pattern of Imports of Blister and Refined Copper for each of the above countries is as follows:

Sources of Imports in approximate percentages

	Total '000 tons	US	Canada	Chile, Peru, Mexico, etc	African Territories, etc	Common Market Countries	Other European Countries
Germany	377	15.2%	1.6%	36.6%	26.6%	14%	6%
Benelux	280	2.0%	0.8%	9.3%	70.0%	6.2%	11.7%
Netherlands	26	18.0%	—	1.2%	8.0%	66.0%	7.0%
France	202	16.4%	3.3%	5.6%	33.2%	39.2%	2.5%
Italy	225	23.2%	0.7%	13.1%	42.3%	11.3%	9.4%
UK	501	5.9%	19.3%	25.6%	47.2%	1.4%	0.8%
US	442	—	15.0%	69.0%	13.0%	3.0%	—

continued—

The following table shows the approximate percentage uses of Copper in various forms in the countries of the Common Market and in Britain.

	Germany	Benelux	Netherlands	France	Italy	UK
Semi-finished Products:						
Copper Sheet, Strip and Plate	5.5%	⎫	⎫	4.0%	6.0%	9.0%
Copper Wire and Stranded Wire	43.5%	⎬ 59.0%		40.0%	44.0%	35.0%
Copper Bars, Rods and Sections	4.5%			4.5%	3.0%	3.0%
Copper Tubes	5.0%	⎭	⎬ 74.0%	7.5%	3.5%	10.1%
Brass Sheet, Strip and Plate	8.0%	⎫		7.0%	5.0%	9.0%
Brass Wire	2.0%	⎬ 33.0%		0.5%	1.0%	1.5%
Brass Rods and Sections	12.0%			14.0%	13.5%	13.0%
Brass Tubes	5.0%	⎭	⎭	1.2%	2.5%	2.2%
Other Alloys	2.0%			1.0%	1.5%	3.2%
Castings:						
Bronze	1.5%		⎫	9.5%	3.5%	⎫
Brass	3.5%	(i)		3.0%	2.5%	⎬ 11.0%
Copper and other	5.5%			0.5%	0.5%	⎭
			⎬ 26.0%			
Copper Salts	1.0%	8.0%		4.5%	9.5%	12.0%
Miscellaneous	0.5%		⎭	1.0%	0.5%	

(i) Included in Semi-finished Products.

(4) PLASTICS

The Production of Plastics in the Common Market is increasing rapidly, probably at the rate of about 300,000 tons a year. In 1962, the output of the products of condensation, polymerization, and cellulose derivatives amounted to 2½ million tons, an increase of 500 thousand tons on the total output of Plastics in 1961.

The following Tables show the relation between Production, Import, Export and the figures for Apparent Consumption, for 1962.

Products of Condensation
'000 tons

	France	Germany	Italy	Netherlands	Belgium/ Luxembourg	Total C. M.
Production	113	465	165	62	22	827
Imports:						
Common Market	24	18	24	18	28	
Other	11	14	7	6	12	50*
Total:	35	32	31	24	40	
Exports:						
Common Market	9	66	66	7	8	
Other	8	86	10	16	1	121*
Total:	17	152	26	23	9	
Apparent Consumption	131	345	170	63	53	756

Products of Polymerization
'000 tons

	France	Germany	Italy	Netherlands	Belgium/ Luxembourg	Total C. M.
Production	279	677	383	47	45	1,431
Imports:						
Common Market	39	45	18	44	36	
Other	24	52	17	21	18	132*
Total:	63	97	35	65	54	
Exports:						
Common Market	21	77	53	15	10	
Other	44	192	105	27	3	371*
Total:	65	269	158	42	13	
Apparent Consumption	277	505	260	70	86	1,192

* Excluding intra-Community Trade

continued—

Cellulose Derivatives
'000 tons

	France	Germany	Italy	Netherlands	Belgium/ Luxembourg	Total C. M.
Production	49	115	34	8	na	206
Imports:						
Common Market	2	3	5	5	5	
Other	3	7	6	2	1	19*
Total:	5	10	11	7	6	
Exports:						
Common Market	4	9	3	7	4	
Other	11	20	1	2	3	37*
Total:	15	29	4	9	7	
Apparent Consumption	39	96	41	6	na	188

* Excluding intra-Community Trade

As between 1962 and 1963 the Export and Import figures increased by the following percentages:

	France	Germany	Italy	Netherlands	Belgium/ Luxembourg
Imports	43%	10%	26%	4%	25%
Exports	30%	20%	—	20%	20%
Imports	30%	—	30%	15%	20%
Exports	45%	18%	7%	20%	70%
Imports	37%	30%	—	85%	40%
Exports	15%	10%	—	8%	15%

(5) PULP AND PAPER

The following Tables give a statistical picture of the Pulp and Paper Industry of the Common Market, with some comparative figures for other countries.

1. *PULP*

Production and Apparent Consumption

	Common Market	US	Canada	Norway, Sweden, Finland	UK
Production ('000 tons)	3,074	22,796	10,360	10,139	200
Apparent Consumption ('000 tons)	5,573	na	7,963	5,510	2,407

2. *PAPER AND BOARD*

Production ('000 tons)	9,684	32,391	8,103	5,714	3,954
Apparent Consumption ('000 tons)	11,483	na	2,463	1,705	5,316

The following Tables show the Common Market Imports of Pulp and Paper and the principal sources of supply.

PULP

Tons

		Principal Sources		
	Total Imports	Norway, Sweden, Finland	US	Canada
Mechanical Pulp	412,711	390,000	neg	neg
Chemical Pulp:				
Dissolving Grades	412,081	223,013	109,393	2,717
Sulphate unbleached	677,347	526,071	21,706	18,416
Sulphate bleached	1,057,450	662,483	26,380	14,362
Sulphite unbleached	436,651	333,929	2,808	12,009
Sulphite bleached	739,263	533,588	45,488	19,548

continued—

PAPER

Tons

	Total Imports	Principal Resources			Intra-Community
		Norway, Sweden, Finland	US	Canada	
Newsprint	655,388	484,590	3,103	12,632	87,366
Other Printing Paper:					
Uncoated	408,386	247,416	2,755	1,092	76,756
Coated	80,239	8,156	13,417	—	47,385
Kraft Paper	990,571	804,373	132,519	5,033	20,256
Cigarette Paper	655	—	—	—	563
Machine-made Paper and Paperboard	610,916	325,107	34,162	1,712	173,783
Building Boards	313,353	174,775	2,311	—	96,523
Other Coated Paper and Paperboard	113,826	37,755	7,586	neg	45,000

(6) CONSUMER DURABLES (Domestic and Office Machinery)

The following Tables show approximate current Production Imports and Exports in the Common Market countries for a number of important commodities.

	France	Germany	Italy	Netherlands	Belgium/ Luxembourg	Total Common Market
Domestic Refrigerators						
Production '000 units	850	1,900	1,750	—	10	4,510
Imports '000 units	274	56	31	289	148	798
Exports '000 units	139	488	603	2	41	1,273
Electric Washing M/cs						
Production '000 units	612	1,105	511	180	133	2,541
Imports $ '000 value	11,060	7,240	9,947	14,558	6,944	49,749
Exports $ '000 value	7,030	42,085	10,662	3,155	1,308	64,240
Radio Receivers						
Production '000 units	2,675	4,000	950	na	1,100	8,725
Imports '000 units	435	1,500	143	1,960	302	4,340
Exports '000 units	602	1,570	173	1,696	1,055	5,096
Television Sets						
Production '000 units	992	1,750	750	na	304	3,796
Imports '000 units	46	33	52	na	14	145
Exports '000 units	19	379	17	na	151	566
Office Machinery Typewriters						
Production '000 units	na	1,400	1,400	375	na	na
Imports '000 units	146	95	44	70	58	413
Exports '000 units	21	614	472	463	5	1,575
Electronic Calculating M/cs						
Imports units	561	1,188	4	298	385	2,436
Exports units	253	21	101	487	2	864
Punched Card M/cs						
Imports units	6,805	11,420	823	2,294	2,487	23,829
Exports units	6,963	3,431	1,130	964	814	13,302

(7) LEATHER FOOTWEAR

The following Table shows the figures for the approximate production, imports and exports of Leather Footwear in the Common Market countries, including intra-Community trade.

million pairs, 1963

	Approximate Production	Imports	Exports
France	105	7	23
Germany	115	31	7
Italy	95	0.6	57
Netherlands	22	10	5.6
Belgium/Luxembourg	13	10	5.4

It highlights the importance of exports of Footwear to the Italian Footwear Industry which sells more than half of its total production in other markets.

Of Italy's exports:

> 22,000,000 pairs are sold in other Common Market countries.
> 18,000,000 pairs are sold in the US.
> 4,700,000 pairs are sold in the UK.
> 3,200,000 pairs are sold in Sweden.
> 2,500,000 pairs are sold in Switzerland.

Against these exports, Italy imports:

> 10,000 pairs from the US.
> 28,000 pairs from the UK.

The second largest exporter of footwear in the Common Market is France.

Her exports are made up as follows:

> 6,300,000 pairs are sold in other Common Market countries.
> 12,000,000 pairs are sold in Associated Overseas Territories, mainly North Africa.
> 2,000,000 pairs are sold in the UK.
> 1,500,000 pairs are sold in the US.

(8) STOCKINGS

The following Table shows the figures for Production, Exports and Imports of Stockings.

Million Pairs

	Production	Exports	Imports
France	324	22	33
Germany	551	43	31
Italy	300	161	3
Netherlands	69	13	41
Belgium/Luxembourg	46	19	37

Of Italy's exports of 161 million pairs (more than half her production), 69 million pairs are sold to other Common Market countries and 83 million pairs to third countries of which the US bought 1 million pairs and the UK bought 24 million pairs.

(9) KNITWEAR

Clothing

The Knitwear Industry of the Common Market countries shows, for Knitted Outer and Underwear, the following contrast between exports and imports (all countries, including intra-Community trade).

Exports $ million   317
Imports $ million   196

When the figures are extracted for exports and imports with other than Common Market countries, the proportion of exports to imports shows a much greater difference.

Exports $ million   148
Imports $ million   30

Thus, in trade in Knitwear with third countries, the Common Market exports five times the value of its imports, with Italy far in the lead with exports at $ million 107 against imports at $ million 5.5, an export:import ratio of nearly 20 to 1.

SOURCES OF STATISTICAL INFORMATION
USED FOR THE COMPILATION OF THESE TABLES

The 1958 Inter-Industry Relations Study
        US Department of Commerce, Washington D.C.

Trade by Commodities: Exports 1963 (O.E.C.D.)

Trade by Commodities: Imports 1963 (O.E.C.D.)

The Non-Ferrous Metals Industry 1963 (O.E.C.D.)

Commerce Extérieur: Tableaux Analytiques: Importations 1963 (E.E.C.)

Commerce Extérieur: Tableaux Analytiques: Exportations 1963 (E.E.C.)

Statistiques Industrielles (E.E.C.)

Bulletin Général de Statistiques (E.E.C.)

Tableaux Entrées-Sorties pour les Pays de la C.E.E.
        Office Statistique des Communautes Européennes